Monaco

Monaco

BY MARTIN HINTZ

Enchantment of the World
Second Series

Children's Press®

A Division of Scholastic Inc.

NEW YORK   TORONTO   LONDON   AUCKLAND   SYDNEY
MEXICO CITY   NEW DELHI   HONG KONG
DANBURY, CONNECTICUT

Frontispiece: Narrow street in Monaco-Ville

Consultant: Amy J. Johnson, Ph.D., Assistant Professor of History, Berry College,
        Mount Berry, Georgia

Please note: All statistics are as up-to-date as possible at the time of publication.

Book production by Herman Adler Design

Library of Congress Cataloging-in-Publication Data

Hintz, Martin.
  Monaco / by Martin Hintz.
  p. cm. — (Enchantment of the world. Second series)
Includes bibliographical references and index.
  ISBN 0-516-24251-2
1. Monaco—Juvenile literature. [1. Monaco.] I. Title. II. Series.
    DC945.H56 2003
      944.9'49—dc22   2003014800

Acknowledgments

The author wishes to thank all the Monégasques he met while visiting their wonderful country: parking-lot attendants, tour guides, priests, palace guards, shopkeepers, ticket takers, restaurant workers. They were all friendly, helpful, and full of ideas of what to see and do. They certainly are People of the Sun.

He would particularly like to thank the staffs of the Monaco Government Tourist Office, particularly Emily Lyons, and the Consulate General of Monaco for their suggestions, advice, and keen observations. Another special nod goes to Vicki and Tom Nelson and their family for the hospitality shown while visiting their home in La Croix Valmar, in southern France. In addition, Vicki's extremely helpful preliminary research, suggestions, and ideas on what to see and do in Monaco helped kick-start this project and kept it in focus.

Without the fluent French-speaking ability of his wife, Pam Percy, the author would not have gotten past the first item on any menu between Saint-Tropez and Monte Carlo's Place du Casino.

As they say in Monaco, "*merci*" (French), "*thank you*" (English), "*grazie*" (Italian), and "*merci*" (Monégasque).

To my wife, Pam. Her encouragement, support, and wonderful willingness to travel anywhere, anytime, keeps the creative process on track.

Contents

Cover photo:
Monaco Harbor
at dusk

CHAPTER

Monte Carlo Casino

Princess Grace Dance Academy performers

Hello,
Monaco

Meet Monaco, the second smallest country in the world but one with such a large personality that it out-distances its dimensions. Sun-drenched stones tumble down to the deep azure sea. Mild temperatures are scented with the perfume of rose gardens, herbs, and exotic plantings. Ancient buildings doze under the brilliant blue sky. Trolleys packed with camera-toting tourists scoot like caterpillars along the avenues. Bankers and other financial experts scurry in their business suits from modern office buildings to open-air restaurants for important business luncheons.

Elegant jet-setters loll on the fancy terraces of their rented apartments, waiting for the nightclubs to open so they can dance away the evening. Movie and recording stars try to hide behind dark glasses and little makeup. Even the modern statues in the green space fronting the 1860s-era Monte Carlo Casino don't look out of place. All of their contemporary steel beams and bright paints make an interesting contrast to the wedding-cake design of the venerable gambling hall.

This is Monaco, where art, business, good eating, festivals, swimming, boating, conversation, and creativity come together in a magnificent swirl. Barely half of the size of New York's Central

Opposite: **The Mediterranean Sea meets the shore of the Principality of Monaco.**

Sailors prepare for a day of sailing off the coast of Monaco.

Park, Monaco packs a giant bundle of romance and adventure into its narrow, cliff-hugging urban stage setting. On the Avenue Saint Martin or the Rue Princesse Caroline are heard an interesting variety of languages within a few feet (meters) of each other. There is the all-pervasive French as well as English, Polish, Arabic, Italian, Japanese, Spanish, German, and a dozen others—all chattering at once.

Compact Monaco

Since Monaco is so compact, it's possible to take in most of it in a single day. At least on the surface. At the end of the day, relaxing in a seaside café over a delicate meal of zucchini flowers stuffed with truffles (*les fleurs de courgette aux truffes*) is most welcome. After such a meal, it doesn't seem so bad to lose a few euros in the casino. Or, instead, take a tour boat from the harbor and peer beneath the surface of the deep Mediterranean. There is also the option to visit the Oceanographic Museum and see hundreds of fish species swimming in the special tanks. Any extra hours in a visit also allow for more exploration of the city's neighborhoods, each with its own charm and personality: Monaco-Ville with its Grimaldi Palace and the Cathédral of the Immaculate

Princely Palace in Monaco-Ville

Conception; Fontvieille and its Louis II Stadium; La Condamine and the port; Monte Carlo and the Opera House; the homes and apartments on the heights of Moneghetti; and the Larvotto beaches.

How about cheering during a soccer (they call it football) championship in the stadium or admiring the pros in a golf competition at the Monte Carlo Country Club? There's oohing and aahing at an international magic competition or at fireworks exploding high over the harbor. Even the breeze seems musical, carrying the strains of classical, jazz, folk, and blues from the clubs and the concert halls.

There is so much to do and see in Monaco. Be sure to cover your ears during the noisy roar of high-performance auto engines at the Grand Prix, but allow your eyes to feast on a princely collection of antique cars. Then, for good measure, check out the size of Napoleon Bonaparte's hat in the palace's Napoleonic Museum. Kids hope that the dozens of porcelain dolls displayed in the Monaco National Museum will come alive and tell their stories. Relax in stately splendor and have a fabulous, but expensive, supper in the Imperial Salon at the Hôtel de Paris, which opened in 1864. Emperors, dukes, princes, kings, actors, prime ministers, and other dignitaries have stayed in its plush surroundings. Pleasing to the eye and sensuous to the nose, perfumed bouquets of flowers soften the impact of the white linen tablecloths and valuable platewear.

Grimaldi Rule for 700 Years

For 700 years, the Grimaldi family has ruled this little bit of European rock and had a part in world history. They capitalized on Monaco's crossroads locale on the northern shore of the Mediterranean to create a financial empire on a site where cultures have come together for more than a thousand years. Over the generations these princes and princesses have held on to their elevated positions among the most "beautiful people" of Europe. Yet they still turn out for folk spectacles, participate in traditional religious ceremonies, are involved in sports, and are regularly seen on the streets of their city. They have been soldiers, scientists, explorers, sailors, business leaders, and peacemakers.

Leading a nation of barely 5,000 citizens, the Grimaldis have taken their tiny nation

The Grimaldi family has ruled Monaco for 700 years. Here Prince Rainier III is surrounded by his family.

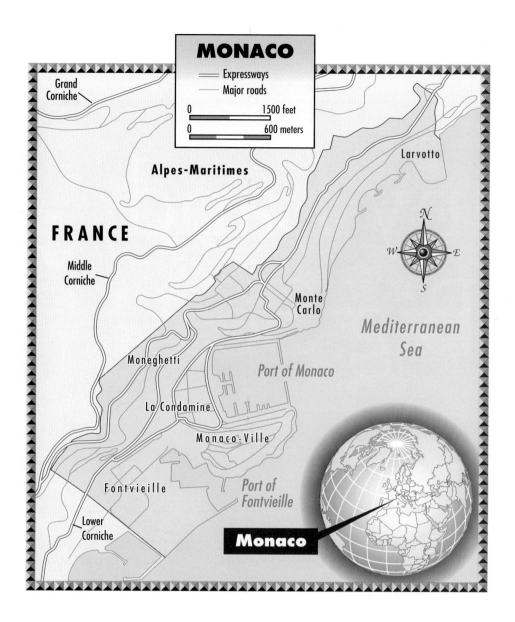

through centuries of unrest. Some have done a better job of governing than others, but Monaco has survived them and moved on. The country has also outlasted sieges and made it through wars and occupations yet retains its expansive, wonderful Old World charm and enthusiastic outlook on life.

Tiny Land,
Big Sea

ON A GOOD DAY IN MONACO—WHICH IS ALMOST EVERY day if you're counting all the wonderful sunshine—a determined hiker can walk across the country in several hours. The time it takes depends on how many stores the stroller visits along the way, how long it is necessary to wait for traffic when crossing a street, and how many stops are made for ice cream. Take good shoes, because this is an up-and-down country.

Such an outing is possible because Monaco is truly tiny. It is the second smallest nation in the world, just above Vatican City in Italy, where the pope, the head of the Roman Catholic Church, lives. Monaco encompasses 0.76 square miles (1.97 square kilometers), whereas Vatican City is merely 0.2 square miles (0.52 sq km). Monaco's land frontier with the surrounding French department of the Alpes-Maritimes runs 2.73 miles (4.4 km). (A department is similar to a state in the United States or to a province in Canada.) The Mediterranean Sea makes up Monaco's eastern boundary and France its western.

The county is a rugged pile of stones, with its buildings clinging to the hillsides

Opposite: **Monaco is built upon steep, rocky cliffs.**

This hotel is perched directly on a cliff's edge.

Monaco's Geographical Features

Lowest Elevation: sea level

Highest Elevation: Mont Agel, 459 feet (140 m)

Average Temperature: January, 50°F (10°C); July, 80°F (27°C)

Average Precipitation: less than 2 inches (5 cm) per month during the winter

Distance East to West: varies between .65 miles (1.05 km) and 382 feet (116 m)

Coastline: 2.55 miles long (4.1 km)

Border with France: 2.73 miles (4.4 km)

Latest Addition: a $328 million floating breakwater adding 15 acres (6 ha) to Monaco's harbor; work began in 1999 and is due to be completed in 2007

in a picturesque tumble-jumble. Monaco tilts at a 45-degree angle away from the Mediterranean, giving a hang-on-tight feel to structures on the cliffs.

Monaco's Neighborhoods

Monaco is divided into six principal neighborhoods. Since Monaco could not grow to the north, it reclaimed 100 acres (40 hectares) of land from the Mediterranean to build up the district of Fontvieille. The Port of Fontvieille, the sports stadium, and a helicopter terminal are located on the seafront, directly below the palace. Monaco-Ville is the oldest section of this ancient town, dating from the Middle Ages. It is built on what the locals call The Rock (*Le Rocher*), rising more than 197 feet (60 m) above the sea. This part of town includes narrow, picturesque streets and alleyways. Monaco-Ville is home to the Oceanographic Museum, the cathedral, and the Princely Palace, where Prince Rainier III lives and has his seat of government. Monaco-Ville is Monaco's capital.

Monaco-Ville was built on the site of a thirteenth-century fortress.

Moneghetti is along the highest part of Monaco, with many monumental apartments and condominium buildings providing amazing views of the blue sea. The famous Exotic Garden (*Jardin Exotique*) is one of the district's primary landmarks with its array of desert plants. Larvotto is a narrow stretch of land on the northeast end of Monaco, where beaches and the Monte Carlo Sporting Club along the Avenue Princesse Grace can be found.

La Condamine consists of the Port of Monaco, with many stores where a determined shopper can find everything from fancy jewelry to antique chairs. Some of the city's best restaurants are here as well. Tourists are always on the lookout for film stars and other notables who visit the neighborhood. Mount Charles (*Monte Carlo* in Italian, *Mont Charles* in French) is the glitzy casino district of Monaco, where time is irrelevant and the gaming goes on day and night. The area received its name in the mid-nineteenth century by Prince Charles III, who authorized the country's first gambling hall. Monte Carlo is the most popular section of Monaco, with the most expensive hotels.

La Condamine market was first opened in 1880. Fresh produce and local specialties can be bought here.

A system of public lifts (elevators) hauls pedestrians up and down Monaco's steep, stony landscape. Six lines of the Monaco Bus Company crisscross the city. After 9 P.M., however, when the buses stop, people needing a ride home or to their hotel catch taxis. Motor coaches also run from Monaco to the surrounding French countryside.

The parallel roads that travel along the heights overlooking Monaco are called *corniches*. The Lower Corniche, (*Corniche Inférieure*) descending from the cliffs into Monaco itself, is one of the most beautiful roadways in the world.

Automobiles wind down a corniche high above Monte Carlo.

The road curves along the coastline for 20 miles (32 km). It runs directly below the busy Middle (*Moyenne*) Corniche, a 19-mile (30-km) stretch of modern highway linking the French town of Menton to the city of Nice. Even higher than the Middle Corniche is the Grand (*Grande*) Corniche, which is also 19 miles (30 km) long, on the heights far above the sea. This road was originally an ancient pathway. The Grand Corniche overlooks Monaco and the Mediterranean, which lies 1,476 feet (450 m) below.

Although Monaco doesn't have a lot of landmass, it does have the Mediterranean. Monaco's maritime holdings extend 12 international nautical miles (22 km) out into the water. An inland sea, the Mediterranean, has been one of the most important bodies of water in the world for many centuries. Its name comes from the Latin words *medius* and *terra*, meaning "middle of the land." The sea separates the continents of Europe and Africa and touches on Asia. But more than keep-

The Mediterranean is an inland sea that connects all the countries touching its waters.

ing them apart, the Mediterranean unites Monaco, France, Italy, and all the other countries on its shores. The term "Mediterranean" has come to mean the people, the geography, the climate, and the plant and animal life affected by its waters. For thousands of years the sea has been used for commerce, recreation, and industrial purposes.

Extensive Mediterranean Waters

The Mediterranean runs 2,200 miles (3,541 km) in an east-west direction and can be up to 1,200 miles (1,931 km) north to south. Almost a landlocked body of water, the Mediterranean's link with the Atlantic Ocean is through the Strait of Gibraltar, a passageway between Spain and Africa only 8.75 miles

(14 km) wide. The water spreads over 1 million square miles (over 2 million sq km) and can be up to 1,313 feet (400 m) deep.

Monaco is blessed with a warm Mediterranean climate that is mild throughout the year. Frosty north winds are blocked by the French Alps, and gentle southerly breezes drift in from the sea. The weather is mild in winter and pleasingly warm in summer. Temperatures in January hover around 50° Fahrenheit (10° Celsius) and 80°F (27°C) in July, but they can soar higher.

Monaco usually has more than 300 days of clear, blue skies and bright sun every year. Summer days with twelve hours of sunshine are typical. Residents love relaxing over leisurely meals in the city's outdoor cafés during the warm-weather months. In January and February, the two coolest months, there is an average of five hours of sunshine per day. Less than 2 inches (5 cm) of rain per month falls during the winter, but that amount is enough to cool the temperatures. Yet only a sweater or a light jacket is needed, even on the coldest days. The country averages barely sixty rain days a year. Nobody ever talks of snow, except for skiing vacations in the mountains.

The mistral is a wind that blows across the Mediterranean from North Africa. It gusts constantly through the year but is strongest in the winter, carrying desert dust from the Sahara. Some jokesters say the mistral can blow the ears off a donkey, although Monaco is not as severely affected as some nearby regions of France and Italy. According to a legend of the Monégasques (citizens of Monaco), the mistral blows only on odd-numbered days of the month.

Polluted Sea

Parts of the Mediterranean Sea are now among the most polluted bodies of water on earth. Raw sewage, oil, detergents, and mercury contaminants affect the water quality, especially along the North African coast. Concerned about what he was observing, Prince Rainier III formed the International Marine Radioactivity Laboratory in 1961 to help monitor water conditions. Fortunately, Monaco has excellent water-treatment facilities.

Gardens and Wildlife

BECAUSE MONACO IS TOTALLY URBANIZED, IT DOES NOT have any forests, pastureland, or wild areas. Nor does it have any native animals beyond several rare species of bats. Eons ago, however, animals did roam the Mediterranean coastline that now encompasses Monaco. In 1902 Prince Albert I founded the Anthropological Museum to house his amazing collection of fossils and prehistoric skeletons. Many of the artifacts were found in the Grimaldi Caves on the Italian frontier, part of the Grimaldi family lands centuries ago. Other bones were discovered in the Gardens of Saint Martin (*Jardins Saint-Martin*) and the deep grotto of the Observatory Caves. The museum is home to the bones of long-extinct animals, including the ancestors of today's rhinoceros, elephant, and reindeer. Today the only animals remotely looking like these remains would be in the exciting acts of the touring Monte Carlo Circus.

Prince Rainier III loves animals and established the Zoological Garden in 1954 after a visit to Africa. The exhibits focus on such tropical animals as monkeys, which live in enclosures with a grand view of the Mediterranean. The zoo also holds a hippopotamus named Polux,

Opposite: **The location of Monaco does not afford it large open spaces; therefore lavish gardens are highly valued.**

A hippo at Monaco's Zoological Garden

Antu the orangutan, Dallas the camel, a tiger called Nina, and two panthers named Pitou and Cirus. There are also exotic birds and reptiles and three bouncy monkeys, Bebe, Casper, and Cruvette. There is a long-standing story in Monaco that if Rainier weren't a prince, he would have become a lion tamer. He does own several dogs and has a mountain farm named Roc Agel, near the Mont Agel Golf Course.

Small dogs are favored and pampered in Monaco.

Pets and Seabirds

Monégasques love their pets and have the usual cats and canines found in a typical metropolis almost anywhere in the world. Well-behaved dogs seem to be everywhere. As do their French neighbors, Monégasques often allow their furry friends to tag along with them into restaurants and shops. Most of the dogs are miniature breeds, with some small enough to be carried in women's purses. These pampered pooches peek out from handbags or snuggle into their owners' arms, gazing at the passing world. The size of the tiny animals is perfect for the extremely small dimensions of Monaco.

Seagulls, terns, and other water-loving birds fly, float, and dive over

Monaco's Mediterranean waters, while land birds include thrushes, doves, magpies, mockingbirds, and sparrows. Dozens of migrating species, from swans to ducks, fly over Monaco each season. They don't stay long before heading south to Africa in the fall and north to nesting grounds in Europe in the spring. A dedicated bird watcher can track their flight in the cloudless sky over the city.

A seagull perches beside a telescope overlooking Monte Carlo.

The Princess Grace Rose Garden contains more than 150 varieties of roses.

There are no huge parks or expansive open spaces in Monaco as with some other countries. There are beautifully landscaped pockets of greenery here and there, however, such as the Casino Gardens (*Jardins du Casino*), Gardens of Saint Martin (*Jardins Saint-Martin*), and the Princess Grace Rose Garden. Space is at such a premium in Monaco that flowers and plants are often cultivated in window boxes or in large pots outside hotels. There is an abundance of hardy olive and umbrella palm trees that make perfect street shading on Monaco's warmer days. A lengthy boulevard, the Avenue of the New Door (*Avenue de la Porte Neuve*), winds down the steep hill from the Palace Square (*Place du Palais*), which is framed with trees whose leaves rustle softly in the Mediterranean breeze. The avenue turns into the shaded Boulevard Albert I, which fronts the Port of Monaco. A children's play area is along the docks where huge yachts are harbored.

The lack of open space and the sometimes-sizzling climate were never problems for dedicated Monégasque gardeners. In the late 1800s Prince Albert I became interested in botany, the study of plants. He wanted to showcase his collection of cacti and other desert plants that grew well in Monaco's hot, dry seacoast climate. He began cultivating these sturdy specimens in the late 1800s and early 1900s. Eventually the prince's work was gathered together to become what was called the *Jardin Exotique* (Exotic Garden). The delightful expanse of floral beauty was inaugurated by Prince Louis II in 1933. The display, which covers 123,786 square feet (11,500 sq m), is precariously perched on Monaco's rugged rocks. The site overlooks Monte Carlo alongside the roadway leading to the nearby French city of Nice. Nearly 450,000 visitors each year come to admire the gardens. Fearless drivers, who need to keep their eyes on the road, can motor along the *Boulevard du Jardin Exotique*. The street runs along the steep hillside crowded with expensive villas and apartments.

Strollers in the garden walk along narrow footpaths and cross bridges to admire the nearly 7,000 cacti and other succulent plants.

The favorable climate of Monaco allows beautiful cacti to thrive at the *Jardin Exotique.*

Monaco's 2,400 to 3,600 hours of sunshine each year contribute to ensuring a healthy, energetic exhibition. The colorful but prickly cacti bloom in the spring and early summer, followed by plants in the *Euphorbia* family showing off in the summer. These cactuslike plants usually discharge a thick, milky fluid if cut. A poinsettia, more commonly found in Mexico and Latin America than in Monaco, is a euphorbia. Its spiky green leaves and red flower-like leaves are used for Christmas decorations. Red and yellow aloes flower next, making Monaco's mild winter alive with rich hues. Native to South Africa, they have thick, fleshy leaves. The fluid from their leaves provides a natural, soothing relief for sunburn and insect bites.

Several garden clubs meet regularly at the Exotic Garden and hold exhibitions. Among the shows is the annual Monaco Expo Cactus, organized by *L'Association Internationale des Amateurs de Plantes Succulentes* (The International Association of the Amateurs of Succulent Plants). The group's enthusiastic members attend lectures and tour the Exotic Garden to pick up gardening tips.

Although Monaco lacks wild space, it has a long, rich tradition of underwriting scientific studies. The nation belongs to international organizations that protect the environment and the world's natural habitats. Among them, Monaco supports the Scientific Committee for Oceanic Research, the International Union for the Conservation of Nature, the International Union of the History and Philosophy of Sciences, and the International Union of Biological Sciences.

Dedicated to Science

Credit for much of Monaco's interest in science can be attributed to the scholarly yet adventurous Prince Albert I (1848–1922). As a child, Albert was fascinated by ships and the sea. In 1866, his father, Charles III, sent the eighteen-year-old Albert to train in the Spanish navy, where he learned how to sail and command a ship. Four years later, Albert joined the French navy and fought in the Franco-Prussian war, earning the rank of lieutenant. When a civilian again, Albert purchased a 200-ton yacht he called *The Swallow* (*L'Hirondelle*) and set out to sea in 1873. His interest in the ocean quickly turned from sailing to science.

He converted *The Swallow* into a scientific research vessel, exploring the Mediterranean Sea and the Atlantic Ocean. When Charles died in 1869, Albert began building ships. He put them all to good use himself, sailing on dozens of research expeditions between 1885 and 1915.

Albert's accomplishments included developing the oceans' first depth charts. He also studied migration patterns of marine life and currents, collecting hundreds of specimens in order to examine the effects of light penetration in the sea. He was an avid photographer who carefully documented his travels. In 1906 Albert established the Oceanographic Institute of Monaco. Always fascinated by the secrets of the sea, in 1910 he built the ornate Oceanographic Museum (*Musée Océanographique*) on an outcropping along the Monaco coast called The Rock (*Le Rocher*). In his inaugural address for the Oceanographic Museum, Prince Albert I declared, "I am opening the Oceanographic Museum to give to the servants of

scientific truth. There they will find the peace, independence, and emulation that will stimulate their intellect." Along with King Alphonso XIII of Spain, Albert launched the International Commission for the Scientific Exploration of the Mediterranean. Today the organization has seventeen member countries. In 1971 Rainier III created the Albert I of Monaco Prize for Oceanography to encourage research in maritime science and to honor his famous ancestor.

The country also is a strong backer of such important scientific gatherings as the Convention on International Commerce in Species of Wild Fauna and Flora Threatened with Extinction.

A diver swims with barracuda in the Mediterranean.

Beneath the Sea

Although Monaco is lacking in land, it fronts thousands of square miles of sea, alive with interesting creatures that live underwater. Among the species of Mediterranean fish there are barracuda, stingrays, and small sharks. Professional fishers have passed along the knowledge of which fish should be avoided. When their nets are pulled to the surface, the fishers are very careful when handling their catch, so they are seldom stung by sharp dorsal spines or bitten with jagged teeth. Yet swimmers and amateur fishers may not be as careful. During the crowded summer, when tens of thousands of people flock to the water on their holidays, injuries do occur. However, not all the Mediterranean maritime life is to be feared. Among the more benign types of sea life are tuna, anchovies, sardines, cuttlefish, crab, and lobster, along with sponges and some coral. The fish feed on each other, on algae, or on organisms that drift down to the bottom from the surface.

The Oceanographic Museum is considered to have one of the best aquariums in Europe. It takes up an entire floor of the building, with ninety dimly lit seawater tanks filled with vividly colored fish and displays of living coral. Among the species are the globefish from Sri Lanka (formerly Ceylon) and the Filipino damsel-fish, as well as sea horses, groupers, and sharks.

Several models of oceangoing research ships are displayed, in addition to ocean-related artwork. A large library is full of books on oceanographic expeditions, undersea life, and related subjects. Two exhibit halls are dedicated to temporary exhibits on oceanic themes. Staffers travel around the world to present films and lectures such as "Coral Gardening at the Monaco Aquarium" and "The Micro-Aquarium." Since December 2000, an aquarium called "The Sharks' Lagoon" has attracted visitors to see fish swimming through a living coral reef.

The late, great underwater explorer and scientist Jacques-Yves Cousteau (1910–1997) was director of the Oceanographic Museum from 1957 to 1988. With the backing of Prince Rainier III, Cousteau focused international attention on challenges facing the health and welfare of the world's oceans and underwater ecosystems. From his base at the Oceanographic Museum, Cousteau worked tirelessly to study and protect the world's water ecosystems.

Eels hide behind coral and pottery in an aquarium in the Oceanographic Museum.

Jacques-Yves Cousteau, world-renowned marine biologist and explorer and one-time director of Monaco's Oceanographic Museum

A Long and Rich History

CHAPTER

FOUR

32

THERE IS NOTHING NEW ABOUT MONACO. THE LAND IS age-old, the sea that washes its shore is ancient. Even the Monégasques come from bloodlines lost in history. Humans have lived along this rocky Mediterranean coast ever since men and women learned to walk, make fire, and share crude tools. Monaco's Museum of Prehistoric Anthropology, founded by Prince Albert I in 1902, houses artifacts from those long-ago days. Hundreds of these bits and pieces of history were found in archaeological digs in the Grimaldi Caves on the French-Italian border.

Opposite: **Monaco Palace, as seen by the painter Joseph-Dominique Bressan in 1732**

Artifacts found in archaeological digs are displayed in Monaco's anthropological museum.

One of Monaco's first inhabitants were the Ligurians, warriors who also settled in Provence, France. These are ancient Ligurian ruins in Provence.

Medieval fresco of a Saracen on horseback

The land that would become Monaco is strategically located at prime crossroads in southern Europe. Throughout the early centuries, many kinds of people traveled through the region. Eventually a tribe called the Ligures, or the Ligurians, settled in for a long stay. Noted for their bravery, they were often used as mercenaries by the imperial Roman armies. Mercenaries are soldiers who are hired for their services. When the Roman Empire collapsed, Monaco was overrun by northern barbarians. During the next dozen generations, Monaco was a battleground. Saracens, fiercely brave Muslim warriors from North Africa and Spain, raided the coastline during the early Middle Ages. They soon were in control. In 975 A.D., the French count of Provence drove out the Saracens and incorporated Monaco into his territory.

Genoa Flexes Its Muscles

The Republic of Genoa (in what is now known as Italy) was flexing its commercial and military muscle around the Mediterranean in the late twelfth century. It gradually stretched its power over to Monaco. During a bloody civil war in Genoa, the Guelph families supported the pope. Others, known as the Ghibellines, owed their allegiance to the Germanic Roman emperors who occupied Monaco. By 1215 the Ghibellines had started building the four main towers and the fortifications that form the outer walls of today's palace, eventually home to Monaco's monarchs.

Soldiers led by François Grimaldi, a supporter of the Guelphs, seized the Monaco fortress on January 8, 1297.

The thirteenth-century palace in Monaco

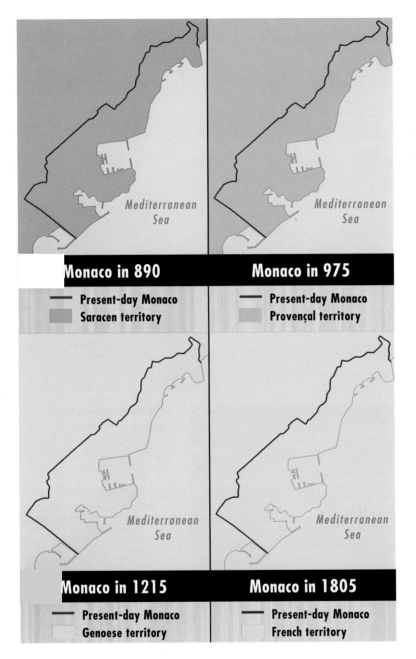

Monaco in 890
— Present-day Monaco
▨ Saracen territory

Monaco in 975
— Present-day Monaco
▨ Provençal territory

Monaco in 1215
— Present-day Monaco
Genoese territory

Monaco in 1805
— Present-day Monaco
French territory

Disguised as monks, they were admitted to the citadel and immediately attacked and killed the Ghibelline guards. Apparently Grimaldi didn't feel bad about this gruesome deception. His nickname was "the Cunning." Four years later however, Grimaldi was chased away by the Genoans reasserting their authority.

During the ensuing years the Grimaldis rose and fell in power struggles over Monaco. They formed an extended family, an *albergha*. Individual princes owned some of the land, while other parcels were shared among the family. There were many alliances with nearby countries and with influential dukes and lords that allowed the Grimaldis to cement their grip over the region. Within the family, as all around Europe, there were relationships that we would consider strange. In the early sixteenth century, one prince married off his daughter to a cousin before she was even fifteen years old. That couple went on to have fourteen children. Marrying a relative, even at a young age, was fairly common during the medieval period. The average life span of that time was barely thirty-five years. Weddings among royalty were more likely to be convenient political unions than marriages of love.

Grimaldis Assassinated

Several Grimaldis were assassinated by rival members of the clan. Eventually a branch led by Honoré I and Honoré II solidified a claim on Monaco in the late 1500s and early 1600s. They were so powerful and respected that Louis XIV of France, "the Sun King," was the godfather to Louis I, a grandson of Honoré II.

Louis I (1642–1701) grew up to lead the family and serve the king of France as a major diplomat. One of his positions was that of ambassador to the Holy See, the jurisdiction or court of the pope. Louis's son, Antoine I (1661–1731), distinguished himself on the battlefield, fighting for France. He was so tall and strong that he was called Goliath. Antoine could wield a conductor's baton as well as a sword. He was a noted musician who led his own orchestra.

Antoine I

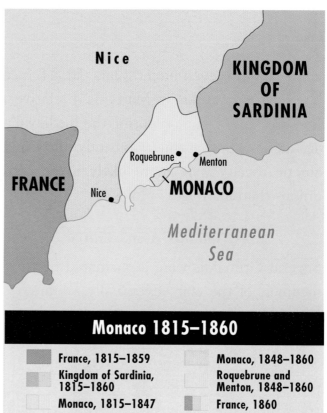

Monaco 1815–1860

■	France, 1815–1859	□	Monaco, 1848–1860
▨	Kingdom of Sardinia, 1815–1860	□	Roquebrune and Menton, 1848–1860
□	Monaco, 1815–1847	▨	France, 1860

Honoré III, prince of Monaco

In 1733 Prince Honoré III became head of the Grimaldis, though he was only thirteen years old! Despite his youth, he worked hard to ensure that the family would stay in power. With the fire and fury of the French Revolution in the 1700s, however, the palace was ransacked, and Honoré III was imprisoned in Paris. He died in 1795 without regaining his authority. It was up to his son, also named Honoré, to retrieve the family titles and lands.

Various treaties returned a portion of the Grimaldi power in the early 1800s, yet the Monégasque princes still had to deal with outsiders. Off the coast of Italy, the island country of Sardinia was given sovereignty over Monaco in the 1815 Treaty of Paris after the defeat of Napoleon Bonaparte at the battle of Waterloo. Although the Sardinians eventually were forced to give up their jurisdiction, things were still not looking good for the Grimaldis. Two towns that they controlled—Menton and Roquebrune—revolted in 1848, proclaiming themselves free cities. With this uprising, the Grimaldis lost about nine-tenths of their territory.

Through the hard-won efforts of Charles III, a treaty was signed in 1861 with Emperor Napoleon III of France. This laid the groundwork for modern Monaco and affirmed Monaco's sovereign status. Among his other triumphs, Charles constructed roads and rail lines and created a customs unit between France and his country. He stimulated Monaco's economy by promoting tourism, established a post office, opened consulates in other nations, and created the first Monégasque stamps.

During Charles III's reign, Monaco expanded its influence along the Mediterranean seacoast. On February 2, 1861, Charles signed a treaty with France giving up claims on the nearby cities of Menton and Roquebrune in order to guarantee Monaco's independence. He also made a payment of 4 million French francs. He oversaw the establishment of the *Société des Bains de Mer* (The Sea Bathing Society, or SBM), which operates the country's casino and several grand hotels in the former Spelugues neighborhood of Monaco. In 1866 the prince ushered through the name change of Spelugues to Monte Carlo.

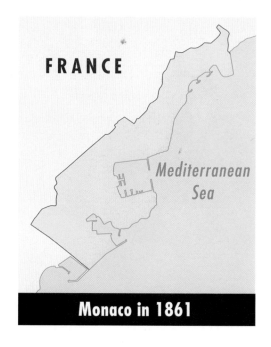

FRANCE

Mediterranean Sea

Monaco in 1861

Prince Charles III established Monaco as a popular tourist area. He opened the rugged coastline to roads and trains.

Wonders of Monaco's Museums

The Monaco National Museum is a showcase of wonderful objects from the country's history. Among the exhibits is a collection of dolls (above) and mechanical figures that young visitors love to observe. Some of the toys date to the early eighteenth century. The museum, located in the Villa Sauber, was designed by the renowned French architect Charles Garnier. An expansive exhibit hall in Fontvieille displays a hundred vintage automobiles from Prince Rainier III's collection. The exhibit traces the development of motor vehicles through the years and how they affected Monaco.

Monaco's Navy Museum is located in Fontvieille, housing an assortment of carefully crafted model boats and nautical objects gathered from around the world (left). Many of the objects are from Prince Rainier's private collection of miniature ships. True to the Grimaldi family's love of the ocean, the displays cover the history of humanity on the sea.

Charles died in 1889 and was succeeded by his son, Albert I. Prince Louis II succeeded Albert I in 1922. During World War I (1914–1918), Louis volunteered to serve in the French army. He won numerous medals for his bravery and earned a general's rank. The current ruler of Monaco, Prince Rainier III, ascended to the Monégasque throne on May 9, 1949.

A Princess for Monaco

In 1953 American actress Grace Kelly visited the Cannes Film Festival in France and was invited to visit Monaco and tour the palace. She found Prince Rainier quite charming, and they stayed in touch by mail and phone. He was invited to her Philadelphia home for a Christmas celebration in 1955, and the couple became engaged. Rainier sent his yacht to America in 1956 to bring

The wedding of Prince Rainier and Grace Kelly

Grace to Monaco for their wedding. More than 1,500 reporters met her when she arrived. On April 18, Rainier and Grace were married in a civil ceremony attended by 3,000 guests.

The next day they were again married in a religious service in the cathedral. It was estimated that 30 million people around the world watched the ceremony on television. In an agreement with MGM, an American motion-picture company, the ceremony was filmed for a movie. The bride and the groom cut the five-tier wedding cake with the prince's sword and then sailed away on the yacht for their honeymoon. Grace had to break her seven-year contract with MGM to become married. Major movie studios of the day usually sought to control all aspects of their stars' lives. This way only the perceived glamour of the stars' lives would be publicized. Subsequently, contracts were often quite restrictive in what the performers could or could not do in their personal lives.

No longer a movie star, Grace Kelly became known as Her Serene Highness Princess Grace of Monaco. She immediately set to work on behalf of her new country. She became president of the Monaco Red Cross and worked for other social and artistic causes. Her movie-star friends flocked to Monaco, which helped the country to again become a fabled vacation locale. Prince Rainier and Princess Grace were among the most glamorous married couples in Europe. In 1957 their first child, Caroline, arrived, followed by Albert and Stephanie.

But the fairy tale ended sadly with the death of the princess from injuries received in an automobile accident on September 13, 1982. Driving with her daughter Stephanie, Grace apparently suffered a stroke that caused her to lose control of the vehicle. She died the next day. Prince Rainier has never remarried.

Despite such challenges, a strong family heritage and the close relationships between the prince and his children ensure that Monaco's future will be bright. Since tradition in Monaco is very important, the royal family will continue to lead the country just as their ancestors had done.

Royal Children

The oldest of Princess Grace and Prince Rainier's three children is Princess Caroline Louise Marguerite (above left). She was born on January 23, 1957. As a young woman, Caroline studied in England and France. After her mother's tragic death in an auto crash in 1982, she took Princess Grace's place in all public duties. In 1990 Caroline's husband, Stefano Casiraghi, was killed competing in a boat race. After a time, she gradually resumed her public and social life, and she married Prince Ernst of Hanover in 1999. Caroline has four children.

Prince Albert's full name is Albert Alexandre Louis Pierre Grimaldi (above center). He was born on March 14, 1958. He is the second child of Prince Rainier and Princess Grace. As a male, he is the heir to the throne. Albert will take over as Monaco's ruling prince when his father either dies or formally retires. Although Albert took his lower-level schooling at the Lycée Albert I in Monaco, he attended college in his mother's home of the United States at Amherst College in Massachusetts.

Following his graduation from Amherst, Prince Albert served in the French navy. After he left the military, he interned in multinational companies in New York to better understand global finance, law, and marketing. Albert loves sports and has a black belt in judo. He is a fencing champion and has played soccer with Monaco's national team for four years. He serves as president of the Monaco Yacht Club, the Monaco Athletic Foundation, and the Monaco Olympic Committee. Although Albert is in his mid-40s and as yet unmarried, Monégasques believe he will someday meet the right woman and make her the new princess of Monaco.

Princess Stephanie Marie Elisabeth (above right), the youngest child of Prince Rainier and Princess Grace, was born on February 1, 1965. She has gone through a variety of careers including fashion designer, model, and photographer. She even launched her own brand of perfume. Stephanie eventually married one of her bodyguards; however, the marriage did not last. Since that time, Stephanie has participated more in public life. In addition to assuming the duties of Monaco's ruling family, she is active in raising her three children.

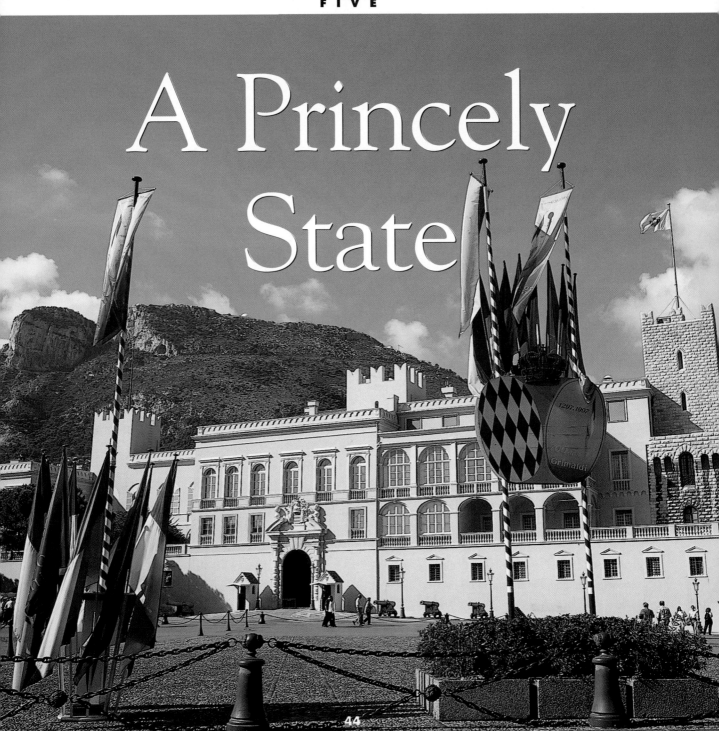

A Princely State

T HE GOVERNMENT OF MONACO IS VERY SIMPLE. THE Monaco constitution, adopted on December 17, 1962, declares that the prince is ruler of Monaco. The Principality of Monaco is a constitutional monarchy. The prince is in charge of everything.

It is important for the Grimaldi family to continue its line of succession. Happily for them, the Grimaldi family line, and the country, Grace and Rainier III had three youngsters: Caroline, Albert, and Stephanie. The princesses now have children of their own. But what determines the line of succession? Who becomes the prince of Monaco when Rainier III eventually dies or retires?

According to Monaco's constitution, succession to the throne is determined by primogeniture (direct descent from the reigning monarch), with priority given to males. This means that the next ruler must be one of the children or grandchildren of the ruling

Opposite: **Flags fly in front of Monaco's Princely Palace, home to Prince Rainier.**

A descendant of Prince Rainier will succeed him to the throne.

Monaco's Prince

Prince Rainier III is a Grimaldi on the side of his mother, Charlotte, who had married Prince Pierre, count of Polignac. His parents separated when he was six, and his father sent him to boarding school in England when he was eight years old. Rainier was very homesick, and he admitted that his time there was difficult, especially because he had to speak English instead of his native French. Rainier toughed it out, becoming a good boxer. He moved on to higher education at Stowe, an English public school. (Public schools in England are known as private schools in the United States and Canada.) Rainier went on to more schooling in Switzerland just as World War II was breaking out.

The young man was called home to Monaco, which was occupied first by the Italians and then by the Germans. He tried studying political science in Paris during the war but again returned home. With the war still raging, Rainier joined the exiled French army in Algeria. As a lieutenant, he was sent back to France and won the *croix de guerre*, one of France's most prestigious medals, for bravery. After the war, he was assigned to the French military mission in occupied Berlin. When his grandfather died, it was Rainier's time to serve his country. In 1949, at the age of twenty-six, he was crowned in the cathedral.

Prince Rainier III has subsequently served one of the longest reigns in Monaco's history. Within that time, he has been active in politics, business, the arts, sports, science, and education. One of his most significant contributions to his country was the development of a new constitution, which was put into effect in 1962. The document updated many of the nation's old laws yet retained its age-old traditions. Rainier has remained on good terms with France. Several French presidents have visited his country for serious discussions on joint issues of finance and security.

To honor individuals who have helped him, Rainier established the Order of Cultural Merit to recognize artistic talent and the Grimaldi Order for services to the state. Rainier still found time to lead all the festivities celebrating his family's 700-year rule of Monaco in 1997.

prince. Primogeniture determines that his successor will be the first-born, or oldest child, except that priority is given to sons over daughters.

How does this affect Monaco? Caroline is the first-born child of Grace and Rainier. Her brother, Albert, is a year younger. By the strict laws of primogeniture, Caroline would succeed to the throne, except that priority is given to sons. Therefore, because Albert is a man, he skips to the head of the line. When Rainier III dies, Albert will become prince of Monaco. However, now in his forties, Albert has never married. Subsequently, under amended rules of succession, if he has no children, his sister Caroline, then her children, her sister Stephanie, and her children follow in order.

Complicated Line of Succession

Assuming that by the time Rainier dies or retires Caroline is also dead, the line of succession passes down through her children. She currently has four youngsters: two boys and two girls. The oldest, Andrea, is a boy and next in line to the throne. But Caroline's next child, Charlotte, is a girl. Therefore, she is skipped momentarily in favor of Pierre, her younger brother. Charlotte would succeed after Pierre and would then be followed by her younger sister, Alexandra.

If none of Caroline's four children are available to become ruler of Monaco, then the line of succession moves over to Princess Stephanie. Her two oldest children, Louis and Pauline, are next in line after their mother. Stephanie has a third child, Camille Marie Kelly, but Stephanie never married the father.

Current Line of Succession in Monaco

1. Prince Albert Alexandre Louis Pierre, the son of Prince Rainier III (born March 14, 1958)
2. Princess Caroline, sister of Albert (born January 23, 1957)
3. Andrea Casiraghi, son of Caroline (born June 8, 1984)
4. Pierre Casiraghi, son of Caroline (born September 5, 1987)
5. Charlotte Casiraghi, daughter of Caroline (born August 3, 1986)
6. Alexandra of Hanover, daughter of Caroline (born July 20, 1999)
7. Princess Stephanie, sister of Albert (born February 1, 1965)
8. Louis Ducruet, son of Stephanie (born November 26, 1992)
9. Pauline Ducruet, daughter of Stephanie (born May 4, 1994)

Under Monaco's laws, because this union was not legitimized by marriage, Camille is removed from the line of succession.

But since there are plenty of Grimaldis ahead in the line, that probably will never be an issue. Assuming that Caroline's oldest son, Andrea, eventually becomes the ruling prince, then the succession will move down through his children.

Branches of the Government

The monarch does not govern alone. In the executive branch of Monaco's government, the prince is assisted by a minister of state and advised by a cabinet. Although the prince is the supreme authority in Monaco, the minister of state is an important position. Whoever holds that job represents the crown. He is second in command and in charge of the country's day-to-day operations, which include commanding the police force, managing the nation's finances, and administering the country's internal affairs. The minister is selected by the prince from a list of three candidates who are French civil servants nominated by the French government through a 1962 agreement with France. Patrick Leclercq was named minister in January 2000.

In addition, the minister is head of the Government Council, which consists of three counselors chosen by the prince who are the heads of departments, or government offices. One is counselor for finances and the economy.

Monaco's Minister of State

Patrick Leclercq, Monaco's minister of state, was born on August 2, 1938, in Lille, France. A career diplomat, he was appointed to his position in 2000 under a system in which France proposes candidates for the top jobs in the principality. As the prince's representative, he has many duties. He manages all executive services, oversees the police, and presides over the Government Council.

Leclercq seems to be everywhere. He has spoken in front of the United Nations General Assembly and has often addressed political and scientific forums held in Monaco.

He served in many foreign countries after graduating from France's *École Nationale d'Administration*, a school of government administrators. When he began his career in the 1970s, he served with the French mission to the United Nations in New York City. Among Leclercq's many important jobs was French ambassador to Egypt (1991–1996) and ambassador to Spain (1996–1999).

Leclercq has received many awards for his service, including the Legion of Honor. He is an officer of the

French National Order of Merit and is a knight of the Order of Saint Isabelle the Catholic. He is married and has three children.

Monaco-Ville: Did You Know This?

The Grimaldi Palace (right), also called the Princely Palace, home of Prince Rainier III in the neighborhood of Monaco-Ville, was once a mighty fortress. In the early 1600s Prince Honoré II (1597–1662) began transforming the building into a true palace. In the late 1690s Prince Louis I constructed a massive gate that still stands as the palace front door. Through the years other design elements were added to the ever-changing castle. Three million white and colored stones, arranged into intricate geometric patterns, make up the

Court of Honor just inside the gate. Chandeliers of Polish glass hang in the throne room. Yet some things have remained the same. Daily, at 11:55 A.M., the traditional ceremonial Changing of the Guard takes place in the Palace Square, an open area fronting the castle. To the rattle of drums, white-uniformed sentries, the *carabinieri*, perform their drills.

Other landmarks in Monaco include the Princess Grace Hospital, which houses an excellent school of nursing within its complex. The Louis II Stadium in Fontvieille, which opened in 1985, seats 20,000 sports fans. A football pitch (soccer field), a sports hall for basketball, a track, and an Olympic-size swimming pool are among its amenities. The elegant Yacht Club at the Port of Monaco hosts numerous racing events on the smooth waters of the Mediterranean. Professional and amateur yachting fans flock here from around the world to demonstrate their skills and to admire the speedy, sleek boats.

The Ministry of State, the offices for many government officials, is housed in a gingerbread-

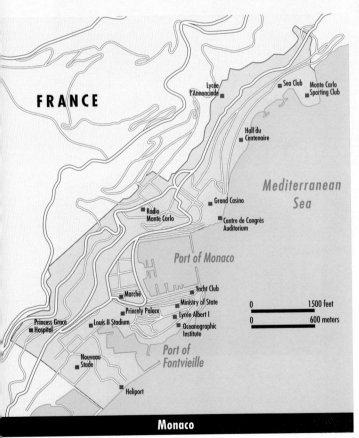

FRANCE

Lycée l'Annonciade
Sea Club
Monte Carlo Sporting Club
Hall du Centenaire

Mediterranean Sea

Grand Casino
Radio Monte Carlo
Centre de Congrès Auditorium

Port of Monaco

Marché
Yacht Club
Ministry of State
Princely Palace
Lycée Albert I
Princess Grace Hospital
Louis II Stadium
Oceanographic Institute

0   1500 feet
0   600 meters

Nouveau Stade

Port of Fontvieille

Heliport

Monaco

style building not far from the Yacht Club and the Lycée Albert I, one of the country's major schools. Monaco's national flags flutter in the warm sea breeze in front of the ministry, making it easy to find.

Monaco is a nation of museums. One of its most noteworthy is the Oceanographic Museum (above), which focuses on everything to do with the sea. Its artwork, scientific exhibits, lecture halls, and fish tanks fill the magnificent structure built on a cliff overlooking the Mediterranean. A major porcelain doll collection fills the halls of the Monaco National Museum. For a touch of really ancient history, the Anthropological Museum showcases the remains of long-ago people who lived along the Mediterranean coast. The palace's Napoleonic Museum houses memorabilia belonging to the fabled French emperor, Napoleon Bonaparte, who conquered most of Europe in the late 1700s. There is even a wax museum that shows off statues of famous personalities from Monaco's rich history.

The Monte Carlo Casino (right) is often simply called "the casino" or the Grand Casino. Often featured in films and novels, the casino brought Monaco to international prominence. In 1864 the casino was merely a small mansion whose main room is today's lobby entrance. The main structure, completed in 1865, is filled with statues of girls picking oranges, boys studying stone roses, and fairy-tale creatures peering out from corners. More gaming can be done at the Monte Carlo Sporting Club, up the coast from the convention center and other tourist attractions.

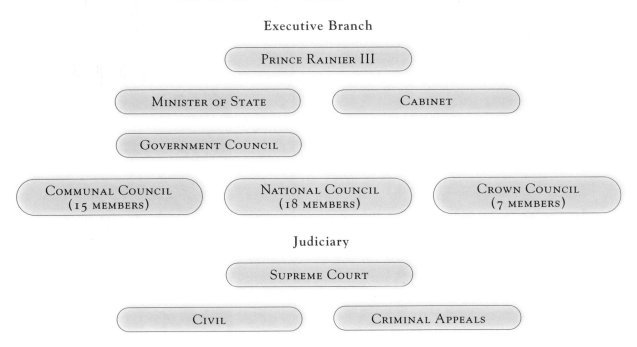

NATIONAL GOVERNMENT OF MONACO

Executive Branch

PRINCE RAINIER III

MINISTER OF STATE

CABINET

GOVERNMENT COUNCIL

COMMUNAL COUNCIL
(15 MEMBERS)

NATIONAL COUNCIL
(18 MEMBERS)

CROWN COUNCIL
(7 MEMBERS)

Judiciary

SUPREME COURT

CIVIL

CRIMINAL APPEALS

Another is counselor of the interior. The third is counselor of public works and social affairs. The Government Council, along with the prince, writes the laws of Monaco and develops an annual budget.

There is also an eighteen-seat National Council (*Conseil National*). Its members are called electors and are directly chosen by the citizens by popular vote. Citizens twenty-one years old and older are eligible to vote. Although political parties do put forth nominees, elections are primarily on the basis of personalities. However, all those elected in 1998 happen to belong to the National and Democratic Union (NDU). Other parties include the National Union for the Future of Monaco and the Rally for the Monégasque Family. Elections are held every five years. In spring 2003 the Union for Monaco party won twenty-one of the twenty-four seats in the National Council. This opposition party trounced the NDU, which had been in power for three decades. The change of hands in the council marked a turning point for Monaco. The reformers wanted their country to reach out more to the rest of the world and supported membership in the Council of Europe. Eighty percent of the country's 5,800 eligible voters turned out for the election.

Although the prince has all of the legislative powers, the government makes sure they are legal. The government also ensures that the prince's directives are carried out after they are signed and published in the *Monaco Journal*. The Government Council can also pass its own laws regulating public service. However, they must be posted by the minister of state. After a ten-day waiting period, the prince can veto a law if he wishes.

The Crown Council

Responsible for requests for citizenship, as well as for pardons and amnesties, the Crown Council must be consulted on international treaties. However, the prince has legal responsibility to represent his country in all world affairs and to sign and ratify any treaties. The Crown Council consists of seven members. Four members are nominated by the prince, and three are designated by the National Council.

Monaco's Flag, the Prince's Standard, and the City's Coat of Arms

castle and take control of Monaco in 1297. The emblem is displayed at the city hall. The country has a former coat of arms (below), with a crown, beneath which are two monks holding swords. The collar around the shield represents the Order of Saint Charles, created in 1858 to honor those who have given important service to Monaco or the prince. The Grimaldi motto, *Deo Juvante* ("With God's Help"), is on the coat of arms, again alluding to the 1297 incident.

The flag of Monaco (above) consists of a red horizontal stripe over a white one. It was adopted during the reign of Prince Charles III, who used the colors from the Grimaldi coat of arms and his personal insignia. Prince Rainier also has his own standard. This is a white flag lined with fringe, flown from his palace and his yacht. In its center is a crown along with his initials.

Monaco's coat of arms is a white shield on which is a painting of a monk holding a sword and a red-checked shield. The man depicts the first Grimaldi, who disguised himself as a priest to slyly enter the local

This does not mean that Prince Rainier III has an easy job, even if he has complete authority over his country. In 1994, Minister of State Paul Dijoud wanted to do away with the traditional system of old Monégasque families always getting the best civic jobs. Two other ministers resigned in protest over his actions, and Dijoud gave up. After a time, running the government returned to normal. Today some younger

Monégasques are confronting the older conservatives who run the departments. The reformers argue for a more modern way of managing the country. For a time, it was thought that the aging Prince Rainier might abdicate, or step down, so that his son, Albert, could take power. Yet Rainier has consistently said he has no intention of leaving, even after he had heart surgery in the mid-1990s.

Because Monaco is both a nation and a city, there are other bodies of authority that are part of the government. The Communal Council (*Conseil Communal*) consists of fifteen persons elected to handle town-planning issues. This group chooses the mayor of Monaco and his or her deputies. On March 19, 1991, the fifteen-member *Conseil Communal* elected Anne-Marie Campora as mayor of Monaco-Ville. She replaced Jean-Louis Medecin, who had held that position since 1971. The mayor presides over the council.

The judges of Monaco's Supreme Court march before the Justice Palace in Monaco.

In addition to his other duties, the prince appoints judges to the Supreme Court (*Tribunal Suprême*). This is similar to the U.S. Supreme Court. The Monégasque legal system is based on French law. The Supreme Court deals with constitutional issues. There are also civil, appeals, and criminal courts. The courts are very strict, with the maximum penalties for crimes usually being handed down. This is done to provide a sense of security for Monaco's tens of thousands of visitors. Of the few crimes in Monaco, most are "white-collar" crimes, involving money issues rather than violence. In 1998 the country's appeals court upheld its first conviction of a person convicted of money laundering. This is an offense in which a

The Monte Carlo police patrol the waterfront.

large amount of illegally obtained money, perhaps made by selling drugs, is given the appearance of coming from a legitimate source.

France is responsible for the defense of Monaco, which does not have an army, an air force, or a navy. Yet Monaco is very safe. There might be a murder every twelve years or so and a few incidents each year of thefts and break-ins. Monaco's police force of more than four hundred officers is considered one of the best-trained in the world. This contributes to the feeling of protection, as does the fact that there is one police officer for about every 100 residents. The police force is managed by a high-ranking French officer and follows a single order given by Prince Rainier. "Monaco must have total security," he proclaimed. Security cameras are everywhere, from parking lots to crossroads. The rich and famous who come to Monaco therefore can feel comfortable wearing their jewels and driving their expensive cars.

Monaco is active in several international bodies, such as the Organization for Security and Cooperation in Europe. When it comes to finances, however, Monaco prefers to go it alone. It does not give out any international aid and does not receive financial assistance from any country. The country is very concerned about protecting the secrecy of its banking system and lobbies to keep its liberal tax system free from European Union regulation. Monaco, however, has applied to be a member of the European Council.

Monaco does not have an embassy in the United States or Canada, but it has a consulate general in New York City. The principality has diplomatic personnel in Germany, the Netherlands, Spain, Belgium, Italy, Luxembourg, Vatican City,

Monaco's National Anthem

	Translation
Principauté Monaco, ma patrie,	Principality of Monaco, my country,
Oh! combien Dieu est prodigue pour toi.	Oh! how God is lavish with you.
Ciel toujours pur, rives toujours fleuries,	An ever-clear sky, ever-blossoming shores,
Ton souvérain est plus aimé qu'un Roi.	Your Sovereign is better liked than a King,
Ton souvérain est plus aimé qu'un Roi.	Your Sovereign is better liked than a King.
Fiers Compagnons de la Garde Civique,	Proud Fellows of the Civic Guard,
Respectons tous la voix du Commandant.	Let us all listen to the Commander's voice
Suivons toujours notre bannière antique.	Let us always follow our ancient flag.
Le tambour bat, marchons tous en avant,	Drums are beating, let us all march forward,
Le tambour bat, marchons tous en avant.	Drums are beating, let us all march forward.
Oui, Monaco connut toujours des braves.	Yes, Monaco always had brave men.
Nous sommes tous leurs dignes descendants.	We all are their worthy descendants.
En aucun temps nous ne fûmes esclaves,	We never were slaves,
Et loin de nous, régnérent les tyrans,	And far from us ruled the tyrants,
Et loin de nous, régnérent les tyrans.	And far from us ruled the tyrants.
Que le nom d'un Prince plein de clémence	Let the name of a Prince full of clemency
Soit repété par mille et mille chants.	Be repeated in thousands and thousands of songs.
Nous mourons tous pour sa propre défense,	We shall die in his defense,
Mais aprés nous, combattront nos enfants,	But after us, our children will fight,
Mais aprés nous, combattrton nos enfant.	But after us, our children will fight.

and Liechtenstein. Neither the United States nor Canada has an ambassador representing its interests in Monaco. Those duties are coordinated through the U.S. consul general in Marseille, France. The honorary Canadian consul for Monaco lives in Monte Carlo, with another consul available in Nice. About 120 honorary consuls represent various other nations in Monaco, and seventy countries have full-time professional consuls in the country.

Economic Muscles

MONACO IS IN AN INTERESTING FINANCIAL POSITION. It is small in geography but large when it comes to economics. Tourism and banking have established the country's financial prowess. Any Monégasque who needs a job can easily find one. Workers from France and Italy are also needed to help fill the workforce.

Monégasques have many privileges not enjoyed by other nationalities living in the country. They receive government housing subsidies to protect them from Monaco's soaring property prices. Living in Monaco is expensive. A four-bedroom

Opposite: **Work is not hard to find in Monaco. Here casino staff clean roulette wheels.**

Homes in Monaco are expensive.

multilevel residence in Fontvieille with a swimming pool and harbor access can cost up to $13 million. Even a simpler house costs hundreds of thousands of euros if purchased by a non-citizen. Ordinary Monégasques would never be able to afford those prices. Citizens also have the right of first refusal when it comes to jobs. A Monégasque must be asked if he or she wants to take a particular position before it is offered to a foreigner. Women are equal to men in Monaco, but they only acquired the right to vote in the constitutional changes of 1962.

Life was not always so rosy for the Monégasques, however. For many years Monaco's ruling Grimaldi family spent little time in their homeland. They began to think of themselves as French, although their ancestors were originally from the Italian city of Genoa. The various princes and their families spent months in Paris or at their estates in Normandy and later at Marchais. Their visits to Monaco were sporadic, sometimes no more than two or three times a year. The Grimaldis came back only to check the family income garnered by taxes levied on the local population.

Revolution Threatens

In the early 1800s the Monégasques felt they were being bled dry financially by the ruling family. Most of the population were farmers, tending small plots of land that were hard, dry, and not good for growing crops. But they had to pay the taxes that supported the lavish lifestyles of their monarchs. By 1856, when Charles III came to power, the situation was becoming tense and dangerous. The Grimaldis desperately needed more money to support their huge estates and expensive tastes. But the Monégasques had no more money to give. They were taxed out. Revolution was in the air.

Charles's mother, Princess Caroline, learned how the rulers of the small German state of Hesse-Homberg had pulled themselves out of dire financial straits by allowing foreign investors to construct a gambling casino in their capital. Subsequently Hesse-Homberg made a healthy income off a yearly lease on the casino, as well as receiving a guaranteed percentage of the casino's profits. Caroline decided that this would be the perfect opportunity to ensure the Grimaldis' future.

In the mid-1800s, however, it was not easy to get to Monaco. There were few roads, no airports, and no trains. This was certainly a problem. With the exception of a daily horse-drawn carriage from Nice, France, and unreliable boat service from various Mediterranean ports, the tiny principality was virtually cut off from the rest of the world. If gambling was to succeed, Caroline told her son, the gamblers needed to be able to safely and quickly reach their small country.

A tram makes its way from Nice, France, to Monaco in 1910.

During the next several years, working with international investors who agreed with their new dream of wealth, the Grimaldis found the means to make Monaco a gambling haven. Only France had enough cash to undertake such large and impressive schemes. It cost millions of francs to blast roads through Monaco's rock and to lay train tracks along the edges of the cliffs.

34 MONTE-CARLO — Ensemble du Casino (Demerlé, Architecte). — LL

A rendering of Monaco's grand new casino in the early 1900s.

Casino Completed

Finally everything was in place. In 1863 construction was completed on a luxurious new casino close to the harbor. Hotels and restaurants were built nearby to cater to the expected flood of high-society guests. Wealthy Europeans arrived in great numbers to play roulette and a popular card game called baccarat. Many outsiders built stylish villas so that they would have places to live when they visited the casino. They also wanted to enjoy Monaco's pleasant climate.

The world's best jewelers, clothing designers, and retailers flocked to Monaco to open shops. It was easy for the locals to find work in the construction business or in industries serving the casino and the hotels. Many became servants in the expensive homes. The Monégasques realized that this was much easier than trying to grow vegetables. They really didn't care that they were not allowed to gamble in the casino. That remained a privilege for the rich and famous outsiders, who brought money into the country.

Wealthy Europeans flocked to Monte Carlo to enjoy the new casino.

To help promote the tourism trade, the Grimaldis figured that the growing community around the casino needed a new name. Several were suggested. Among them were *Charleville* and *Mont Charles*, to honor Prince Charles. In 1866, *Monte-Carlo*, Italian for "Mount Charles," was chosen, and a new era for Monaco began. Over the ensuing years, Monaco has enhanced its ability to lure the moneyed class, theater and movie stars, and curious tourists by building more accommodations and entertainment venues. Lobbies in luxury hotels glitter under crystal chandeliers and highly polished brass. The *Société des Bains de Mer* manages the casino and many of the hotels, as well as most of the other leisure facilities in Monaco.

The wealthy chose Monte Carlo for its climate and grandeur.

Casino Place - Coffee-house

It is simple for tourists and businesspeople to visit Monaco. The closest air terminal is the Nice–Côte d'Azur International Airport, which is 15 miles (24 km) to the west in Nice, France. Air time between Nice and New York is about eight hours and around ten hours between Nice and Toronto, Canada. Travelers can make connections from the United States and Canada through Paris, London, Zurich, Geneva, Madrid, and other European cities.

Some well-to-do visitors arrive at the Monaco heliport ferried by Heli-Air Monaco helicopter from the Nice airport. The flight high over the Mediterranean whitecaps and along the rough coastline takes barely seven minutes. Those who don't need to travel so quickly can get to Monaco by bus, taxi, or rental car. The French National Railroad also serves Monaco, which has an impressive underground train station in La Condamine. The busy rail terminal overflows with brilliant murals and exotic artwork that make waiting for a ride an artistic experience. The trains run frequently to Nice and back—an easy twenty-minute trip each way.

The elegant and historic Hermitage Hotel

The limousine crowd flocks to the 193-room Hôtel de Paris with its sauna and health center. Other wealthy visitors pack the Hermitage Hotel and enjoy its spacious terrace overlooking the blue Mediterranean. The Monte Carlo Grand Hotel, the Beach Plaza, the Mirabeau, Le Meridien Beach Plaza, the Metropole Palace, and other hotels attract repeat visitors. The Monte Carlo Sporting Club on the Avenue Princesse Grace and similar havens for night-owl partygoers are packed. Patrons cheer rows of high-stepping dancing girls. Gourmet restaurants with multipage menus are always crowded, while world-famous chefs create masterpieces. With their booming musical beat and flashing strobe lights, discos such as Jimmy's aim for the younger dance set.

Monaco has constructed an International Conference Center and the Monte Carlo Convention Center-Auditorium catering to large well-paying convention groups and trade shows. These facilities have all the meeting and dining space necessary for large groups. The auditorium seats have special armrests that contain a writing table, microphones, and headphones to hear simultaneous translations. The Grimaldi Forum Monaco was completed in 2000 and offers even greater facilities for meetings, conventions, and cultural events.

The Grimaldi Forum Monaco, opened in 2000, is built on land reclaimed from the sea. Operas, ballets, and meetings take place inside.

Such accommodations are appreciated by event organizers, who know they can stage a program in memorable surroundings. Major corporations and trade associations from around the world such as General Motors, Toyota, Deutsche Bank, the European Petrochemical Association, and Air France regularly use Monaco's meeting facilities.

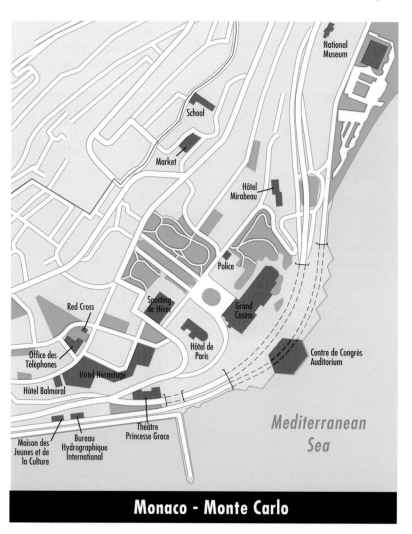

Monaco - Monte Carlo

The original casino, designed by Europe's most notable architects of their day, still stands as part of the country's centerpiece building. Today gambling income amounts to about 4 percent of Monaco's annual revenue. Another big attraction for the world's wealthy has been the absence of an income tax for Monaco's residents, who also are not taxed on their property or inheritances. Corporations pay only very low business taxes. This has created a positive financial climate for noncitizens with homes in Monaco. Among them are the Beatles' Ringo

Putting a Stamp on It

Collectors love Monaco's selection of postage stamps, among the most colorful in the world. Fireworks, bouquets of flowers, fish—just about anything makes a subject for these simple but artistic renditions of Monégasque life. To note Prince Albert's twenty-first birthday in 1979, the postal service put out a stamp with his portrait. The country issued its first stamp, with

the likeness of Charles III, in 1885. Today that small piece of paper is worth thousands of dollars to determined philatelists, or stamp collectors. The government has a monopoly on Monaco's stamps, the sale of which brings a great deal of money into the national treasury.

Starr, tennis great Bjorn Borg, racing champion Michael Schumacher, and opera star Placido Domingo.

Wealth and Industry

All this wealth has made banking an important part of the economy, with more than seventy private financial institutions operating in Monaco. Today both Monégasque banks and branches of foreign-owned financial organizations account for almost 20 percent of the country's business. Monaco is said to provide a secure home for more than 300,000 accounts, with total assets worth more than $40 billion.

In addition, industry is slowly gaining a greater hold in Monaco, representing some 10 percent of the country's income. Almost a sixth of all salaried Monégasques work in the industrial sector, with the manufacture of chemicals, pharmaceuticals, textiles, clothing, cosmetics, and electronics being the major products. Since Monaco does not have any natural resources, all energy and raw materials must be imported. The shipping industry is another growing segment of the economy, with shipping companies sending huge freighters and tankers to world ports from Monte Carlo.

Monaco is now economically healthy. Its unemployment rate hovers around 3 percent, far below the average for other modern nations. In terms of per capita gross domestic product (GDP), a computation of the values of a country's total yearly economic activity, Monaco ranks seventh in the world at around $800 million. It is behind only Luxembourg, the United States, Bermuda, Switzerland, Singapore, and Hong Kong. Taxes on banks as well as on the leisure and commercial sector account for about half of the GDP. Tourism makes up another 25 percent.

Monaco's economy is healthy, and industry is a growing sector in the country.

From its humble beginnings Monaco has risen to be one of the world's economic powerhouses. Yet Monaco is still not totally financially independent. While technically separate, the country is completely tied to the French economic system. Its banking laws are under French regulations. Nor is Monaco a member of the European Union. Customs, postal service, and telecommunications are also managed through links with France.

Tourism accounts for one-quarter of Monaco's GDP.

The Euro

Until January 1, 2002, Monaco used the French franc as its basic unit of currency, and the Italian lira was also widely accepted. After that date the country, like France and Italy, began using the euro, adopted by the European Union as its official currency. No nation now accepts the German mark, the Spanish peso, or other coins and bills that used to be in circulation.

Each euro is worth 100 cents. There are eight denominations of coins, with one side common to all the European Union member countries. National symbols can be used on the back of individual coins.

Monaco's euro coins depict the Grimaldi family coat of arms on its 1-, 2- and 5-cent coins. The family seal is depicted on the 10-, 20- and 50-cent coin. On the 1-euro coin, a double profile of Prince Rainier III and Prince Albert is depicted. The 2-euro coin has the right profile of Prince Rainier III. Euro bills are the same in all the European Union nations that have adopted the euro: France, Germany, Austria, Belgium, Spain, Finland, Greece, Ireland, Italy, Luxembourg, The Netherlands, and Portugal, as well as unaffiliated countries such as Monaco, San Marino, and Vatican City.

Whether Monaco can retain its fast-paced lifestyle is a question being asked by the country's financial experts. To keep up with competition from other parts of the world, Monaco knows it must continue catering to the needs of its guests. Hotels are constantly being refurbished, museums upgraded, and entertainment facilities improved. Linking with the world, there are five French-language television and radio stations, as well as Internet providers. Cable television and satellite dishes are widely available and provide hundreds of channels.

As Monaco moves ahead in the twenty-first century, it needs to continue to be creative in its offerings that attract outside investment and visitors. This really should not be a problem. After all, Monaco has a 700-year history to support its creativity.

Hotels compete with each other to provide their guests with the best service and accommodations.

Tune in to Radio Monte Carlo

Radio Monte Carlo (RMC) is one of the most popular stations in Europe because of its diverse programming. Launched in 1942, it broadcasts news, pop, and classical entertainment and a variety of other shows.

RMC broadcasts in French, Italian, and Arabic to the fifteen countries where most of its listeners live. The station also airs shows in thirty other languages as part of a shortwave radio network reaching around the globe. RMC is now based in Paris. Its first show was hosted by the noted actor Maurice Chevalier.

People from the Land of the Sun

THE "FIRST" MONÉGASQUES WERE VERY DIFFERENT FROM today's residents of the Principality of Monaco. They were prehistoric cave dwellers. During the Paleolithic era, the earliest period of the Stone Age, these early humans hunted, fished, and gathered plants to eat. Small family groups moved often in search of food, roaming up and down the northern shore of the Mediterranean Sea. Their remains have been found in caverns throughout what is today's southern France. Several of these skeletons are displayed in Monaco's Anthropological Museum. When discovered, the remains were surrounded by carefully crafted stone tools.

Successful archaeological digs supported by Prince Albert I led him to create the Human Paleontology Institute, launched in 1910 in Paris. The institute has subsequently been instrumental in uncovering and cataloging other valuable historic finds in Spain as well as in France.

Over the centuries, other people settled down the coast where Monaco is now. Protected from inland attack by the rocky cliffs, they appreciated the site's excellent harbor. Most of these early settlers were hardy sailors, bravely navigating by the stars to find their way across the Mediterranean. Possibly they even ventured

Remains of prehistoric cave dwellers are displayed at Monaco's Anthropological Museum.

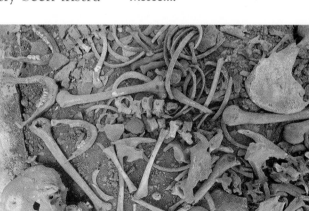

out through the towering Strait of Gibraltar to the vast, uncharted Atlantic Ocean. They attached different names to the lands they discovered, such as the Garden of Oranges, the Islands of the Storm, and the Land of Silver. According to legend, the strip of land that now makes up Monaco was known as the Land of the Sun. Actually, the word "Monaco" derives from the Latin words *Portus Monoeci*, supposedly one of the harbors visited by the mythological hero Hercules on his journeys.

Ancient Monaco

In ancient tales Hercules was the son of the Greek god and goddess Zeus and Alemena. He went into exile and traveled throughout the Mediterranean, accomplishing great feats of strength and bravery. Roman writers Virgil and Lucan referred to the Monaco coast of their time as a calm port as well as a strong fortress. The Roman emperor Caesar is said to have harbored his fleet in Monaco.

Jars from an ancient shipwreck rest on the Mediterranean seabed.

The Phoenicians, Greeks, and many other long-ago peoples are known to have put their historical stamp on this small bit of stony coastline, each adding more ethnic flare to Monaco. Today the waters of the Mediterranean still toss up memories of those long-ago men and women. Skilled scientists searching the waters off Monaco regularly find tarnished coins from Carthage, an ancient North African city. Divers discover beautiful pottery in submerged old shipwrecks and even swords and other armaments, testifying to the area's embattled past.

Population of Monaco

Total population (2002 est.)	32,020
French	47%
Italian	16%
Monégasques	16%
Other (British, American, Belgian)	21%

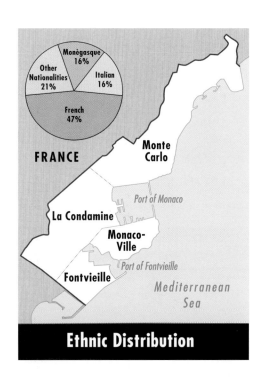

Ethnic Distribution

Being Monégasque

If a non-Monégasque woman marries a Monégasque man, she receives Monégasque nationality. However, she cannot vote or run for office until she has been married more than five years. The population growth rate in Monaco is at merely 0.46 percent a year, with about 10 births and 13 deaths per 1,000 people per year.

Monaco's population grows at a slow rate, though Monégasques live long, healthy lives.

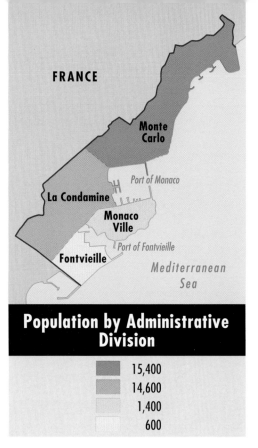

Population by Administrative Division

	15,400
	14,600
	1,400
	600

Above right: **A sign in French proclaims a shortage of gas.**

French is the major spoken language, but a native Monégasque dialect, a combination of French and Italian, is still taught in the schools. However, fewer than 17 percent of

Common Words and Phrases

French	English	Italian	Monégasque
Bonjour	Hello	Buon giorno	Salve
Au revoir	Goodbye	Arrivederci	A se revede
Madame	Madam	Signora	Sciá or Madama
Monsieur	Sir	Signore	Sciu or Monsue
Je m'appelle	My name is	Mi chiamo	Me ciamu
Oui	Yes	Si	Sci
Merci	Thank you	Grazie	Mercí
S'il vous plait	Please	Per favore	Pe pieijé

the population speaks Monégasque, which was almost extinct by the 1970s. English is spoken by almost everyone.

Monégasques are a healthy people. Private health insurance helps them with their medical care. Doctors are trained in France. When locals become ill, they can be treated at the Princess Grace Hospital. The facility also can accommodate noncitizens if they need care while visiting Monaco. The overall average life expectancy of Monégasques is 78.8 years. For men the life expectancy is 75.04 years, while for women it is 83.12 years.

Princess Grace Hospital

A Country of Spirit and Tradition

MONACO REACHES FAR BACK INTO THE DIM PAST TO find the roots of its religious heritage. Over the centuries, this part of the European continent was a meeting point for numerous cultures. Through the ages, the people there worshiped many gods. The Phoenicians built a temple to their god Melkarth, also called Monoicos, on the outcropping of stone on which the current Grimaldi Palace is built. The Romans settled along the coast, believing their many deities would take care of them.

Legend of Dévote

The first evidence of the existence of a Christian community comes at the beginning of the fourth century. In 303 and 304 A.D., the Roman emperor Diocletian began a fearful persecution of Christians. According to legend, among the victims was a young woman named Dévote who lived on the Mediterranean island of Corsica. Unfortunately, the Roman governor of Corsica delighted in arresting Christians and torturing them. Dévote was taken prisoner. But no matter how brutally her persecutors injured her, Dévote stayed true to her faith until, at last, she died.

In order to make sure that Dévote could never get a Christian burial, a Roman official had her body placed in a small wooden craft and cast it adrift, hoping that it would float to North Africa. But soon after the boat drifted from the

Saint Dévote, Monaco's patron saint

Corsican shores, a storm arose. Despite the high seas and howling winds, a beautiful dove emerged from the mouth of Dévote, calmed the waves, and then guided the battered vessel to Monaco's shore. A flowering bush sprang into early bloom where the boat landed.

Another version of the legend says that several fugitive Christians took Dévote's body to sea, hoping to reach Africa and safety. Their ship, instead of going south as they had planned, drifted north and then started sinking. In this story a storm also arose, bringing fear to the sailors. But the spirit of Dévote allegedly appeared to one of the men in a dream. The apparition urged him to follow a dove that would fly from her mouth and lead them to a safe haven. The sailor complied with the instructions. The crew was able to beach the leaking ship, and the girl's body was buried there on January 27.

Whatever the real tale, it wasn't long before local peasants and sailors came to pray at Dévote's grave. Miracles were attributed to her. A thief decided to steal the bones of Saint Dévote and sell them for their powers. Luckily, a group of men fishing nearby saw what he was doing. They saved Dévote's relics and burned the man's boat.

To this day, each January 27 there is a candlelit procession and a special ceremony attended by the royal family to honor Dévote. Doves are released, and a boat is burned to remind

Prince Rainier and Prince Albert set light to a boat during Saint Dévote ceremonies.

Monégasques of the time when their patron saint's relics were almost stolen. The palace, the town, and the sea are all blessed, followed by a huge fireworks display. Many of these ceremonies take place in the courtyard in front of a tiny chapel devoted to Saint Dévote. The church was built in the eleventh century and expanded in 1870, supposedly in the cove where Dévote's ship washed ashore. Today apartments and office buildings hang on the cliffs overlooking the small building, located on the Rue Grimaldi.

The life of Saint Dévote has been immortalized in poems by Monégasque writer Louis Notari (1879–1961). His story about the saint, written and performed in the local dialect, is credited with helping to revive the Monégasque language.

Saint Dévote Chapel

One-Religion Country

Monaco is an overwhelmingly one-religion country, with 90 percent of its residents describing themselves as Roman Catholic. Monaco is an archdiocese, led by an archbishop. Most of the remaining 10 percent of Monégasques belong to various Protestant denominations, such as Episcopalian. Prior to World War II, only a few Jews lived in Monaco. During the Holocaust, the government protected these citizens by faking records that would have revealed their Jewish identity. After the war, several more Jewish families settled in Monte Carlo, primarily as retirees from France and the United Kingdom. In addition, a small number of North African and Turkish Jews have moved to the country.

Monégasques still joyfully celebrate their faith. There are several beautiful churches and historic chapels where they worship. The Chapel of Saint John the Baptist,

Interior view of the
Palatine Chapel

today known as the Palatine Chapel, was built in 1247. One of the newest churches is the Church of Saint Charles, constructed in 1883. Its chandeliers come from the old armory of the palace, which is now the palace throne room.

Other sacred buildings include the Chapel of Saint-Martin. For six centuries, the heart of life in Monaco was the parish church dedicated to Saint Nicholas, the patron saint of sailors, but in 1874 the church was torn down. In its place the Cathédral of the Immaculate Conception was built.

Monaco's Cathedral

Monaco's Cathédral of the Immaculate Conception, located on Avenue Saint-Martin, is a towering structure of white stone quarried from La Turbie in France. The first block of the Byzantine-style building was laid on January 6, 1875, during the reign of Charles III. Massive pillars of granite hold up the roof, and the main altar is made of highly polished Carrara marble. Construction was completed in 1884. Many of the country's rulers are buried in magnificent tombs inside the cathedral. Princess Grace is also buried here.

Valuable artwork in the building helps convey its lofty spiritual message. Among the artifacts is a Spanish altar made of gilded wood dating from the Spanish Renaissance, sixteenth-century paintings, and an abundance of stained glass. A Catholic mass is said in English at 12:15 P.M. each Sunday during July, August, and September.

In 1639, Prince Honoré II laid the first stone of the Chapel of Mercy, which was the main church for the Venerable Brotherhood of Black Penitents, an organization of pious Monégasque men. The chapel's main altar of colored marble was brought from the old Church of Saint Nicholas. In the seventeenth century Prince Louis I built the Convent of the Visitation on the Rock. In the old days, the nuns here were all from royal families, responsible for educating generations of young Monégasque women.

Although Roman Catholicism is the official religion in Monaco, freedom of worship is guaranteed by Article 23 of the Monégasque constitution. Yet there are only a few places for

Monaco's Religions

Roman Catholic	90%
Other Christian denominations	5%

In Monaco, people are free to practice any religion, although the majority are Roman Catholic.

Protestants to worship. Saint Paul's Anglican Church is on the Avenue le Grande Bretagne. The parish has only 135 registered members of more than a dozen nationalities. There is also a Monaco Christian Fellowship that meets regularly in a building on the Rue Grimaldi. While there are a few Jews, Muslims, and people of other faiths living in Monaco, there are no synagogues, mosques, or temples available for their use.

While it is discouraged, there is no law against proselytizing, or trying to gain converts. But religious organizations seeking new members must be registered with the Ministry of State. Some groups considered fringe sects have been denied such permission in the past.

Religious Holidays in Monaco

Feast of Saint Dévote	January 27
Easter Sunday and Monday	March or April
Feast of the Ascension	May 9
Feast of Saint John	June 24
Feast of Saint Roman	August 9
Feast of the Assumption	August 15
All Saints' Day	November 1
Feast of the Immaculate Conception	December 8
Christmas	December 25

Religious Traditions

Religious traditions are integral to the cultural and social heritage of the country. During the sieges of the sixteenth century, the relics of Saint Dévote were carried around the ramparts of the palace. Seeing their patron "protecting" them, the defenders continued to fight valiantly.

Holy Week traditions date back to the Crusades, when Europeans marched off to the Middle East to recover the city of Jerusalem from Muslim rule. Accounts of Good Friday processions in Monaco date back to the thirteenth century and became popular under Prince Honoré II in the 1600s. Each year the Venerable Brotherhood of Black

In Monaco, Saint Roman is honored every August.

Penitents organizes a religious ceremony on this day to remember the death of Jesus Christ. They proceed through the streets of the old city, acting out the Stations of the Cross to recall the various steps Christ took before he was crucified.

After Saint Dévote, Saint Roman is the most popular holy figure in Monaco. Roman was a soldier who was martyred for his faith in the year 258. Marking his feast day on August 9 are dancing and festivities.

On June 23, the eve of Saint John's Day, the prince's family joins the locals in a pageant on the Palace Square. The

Palladiene, a Monégasque folk group, performs in traditional ethnic costumes. After the performances, Prince Rainier, Albert, Caroline, Stephanie, and members of Monaco's trade associations attend mass in the palace chapel. At the end of this ceremony, two members of the household staff light a bonfire in the center of the square. A few brave spectators sometimes jump over the fire.

On June 24 the holiday festivities move from Monaco-Ville to Monte Carlo, with a procession featuring a man dressed as Saint John carrying a lamb. A long line of people

Folk dancers perform to celebrate Saint John's Day.

wind their way from the Place de Moulins through the city streets to the Church of Saint Charles, where there is a religious service. The group returns the same way to the Palace Square where another bonfire is lit, the Monaco national anthem is played, and everyone dances.

Before the long forty days of Lenten fasting that end in the feast of Easter, Monégasques celebrate their Carnival, which dates back to the fifteenth century, giving the people one last chance to party before the period of prayer. Children dress up in traditional clothes and march around the city. Occasionally they stop and hold a large piece of cloth by the corners. Shaking the cloth, the kids toss a straw dummy into the air and catch it again. Carnival also has taken on a more adult, marketable image to attract the tourists. A local club presents a joyful procession with floats, puppets, confetti fights, and dancing, similar to a Mardi Gras procession in other countries such as Canada and the United States.

Rite of the Olive Branch

While the custom is not observed as much in modern times, a Monégasque Christmas of years ago would involve the youngest member of the family dipping an olive branch into a glass of wine. The boy or girl would then go to the blazing fireplace and trace the sign of the cross while saying a poem praising the olive tree. Afterward, everyone would sip from the wine glass before having a meal of *brandamincium*, a traditional Monégasque dish of salted cod prepared with garlic, oil, and cream. Also served would be stuffed fritters and *fougasses*, flat biscuits sprinkled with sugared red and white aniseed. The crunchy biscuits would also be flavored with drops of rum and flowered water.

Also on the Christmas table would be a round loaf of *u pan de Natale*, a Christmas bread on which four walnuts were placed to form a cross surrounded by olive twigs.

Today Monégasques usually attend midnight mass in the cathedral and at least have some of the special holiday bread, even if they don't perform all the old rituals.

Culture and Sports

MONACO HAS ALWAYS PRIDED ITSELF ON BEING A CULtural haven and a sporting mecca. Its royal family has long been a patron of ballet, opera, art, and theater, as well as sporting events of all kinds. When Princess Grace was alive, she used her theatrical and film training to good advantage. With Prince Rainier's behind-the-scenes encouragement, she took the lead in organizing concerts, stage productions, and gallery openings that drew wealthy art patrons from around the world.

Opposite: **Members of the Princess Grace Dance Academy perform at Garnier Hall.**

Foundations Contribute to the Arts

The Princess Grace Foundation was established in 1964 to aid various Monégasque programs. Among its many causes in the medical, social, and arts fields, the foundation supports the Princess Grace Dance Academy, with classes held in a villa called Casa Mia (left). Classes are attended by starry-eyed hopefuls from around the world.

The Prince Pierre Foundation was organized in 1996 by Prince Rainier III in honor of his late father. Its mission is to encourage arts around the world, annually awarding a Grand Literary Prize, the Prince Rainier III Prize for Musical Composition, and the International Contemporary Art Prize.

Even with the death of Princess Grace in 1982, Monaco's entertainment scene remained among the brightest and liveliest in Europe because Prince Rainier III remains interested in the arts. In his late wife's honor, he established several festivals and scholarships to promote painting, sculpture, music, and literature.

The prince was happy to capitalize on his country's long-standing cultural reputation. Since 1879 the Monte Carlo Opera had made its home in the Salle Garnier. This palace of culture is also home to ballet and symphony orchestra

Monte Carlo Opera House

Monaco's Favorite Native Son

Poet and singer Léo Albert C. A. Ferré (1916–1993) was one of Monaco's most famous native sons. He was very active politically, supporting such causes as the Anarchist Movement and the Communist Party.

Ferré's father, Joseph, was director of the Monte Carlo Casino, and his mother, Marie, had a sewing

workshop. When he was nine years old, Léo was sent to Italy for classes, where he became interested in music and poetry. In 1935 he moved to Paris, received a diploma in political science in 1939, and served in the French army. Moving back to Monaco, he began a business as a hotel-forms distributor.

His next job was with Radio Monte Carlo, where he worked as an announcer, a sound-effects engineer, and a pianist. He became friends with notable singers Edith Piaf and Charles Trenet, who suggested he seek work as an entertainer. Taking their advice, he first worked at the Parisian cabaret Beef on the Roof (*Boeuf sur la Toit*) and soon composed a well-respected opera, *The Life of the Artist*.

In 1954 he wrote an oratorio (*Song of the Evil-Liked*) for the Opera Monte Carlo. An oratorio is a long musical composition usually with a religious theme. Ferré recorded many new songs, usually accompanying himself on the piano or the organ. He traveled throughout the world, including trips to Canada in 1965 and 1966. Ferré performed with a French pop group called Zoo, recording an album entitled *Solitude* with it. In the summer of 1975 he went to Switzerland to conduct an orchestra. In the fall he repeated his success in Belgium and France. From 1976 to 1990 he recorded with CBS, then RCA and EPM. Among his most popular songs during this time were "One Is Not Serious When One Is Seventeen Years Old" in 1986 and "The Old Buddies" in 1990.

In 1993, at age 77, Ferré died in Italy after a long illness.

productions. Looking like a magical frosted cake, the building houses both the Opera House and the Casino Cabaret. Over the generations, dozens of famous singers have performed here during the winter. The glorious voice of Nellie Melba drew crowds during the peak of her career between 1890 and 1921. Fabled tenor Enrico Caruso was a regular from 1902 to 1915. Fyodor Chaliapin was always in vogue, enjoying packed audiences from 1905 to 1937. Contemporary performers include Ruggero Raimondi, Luciano Pavarotti, and Placido Domingo.

Monaco's Musical Marvels

Monaco is noted for other musical wonders. The 100-member Monte Carlo Philharmonic Orchestra was officially formed in 1979. It grew out of the success of the country's first symphony orchestra, popular as far back as 1863. Led by Marek Janowski,

Monte Carlo Philharmonic Orchestra

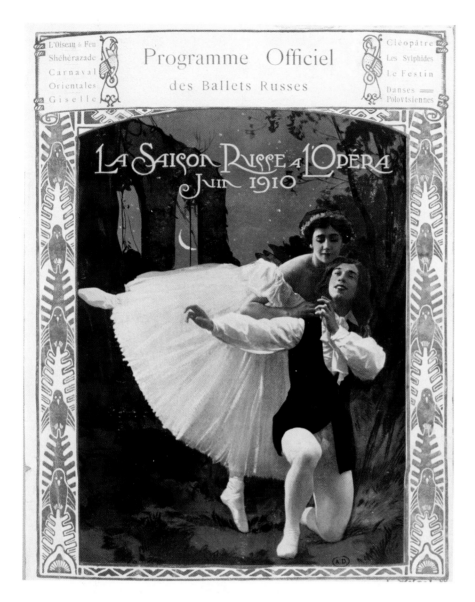

A program from the 1910 performance of *La Saison Russe a l'Opéra*, featuring Vaslav Nijinsky.

the philharmonic holds concerts all year. Some are presented in the palace's main courtyard.

Like other musical presentations, dance is nothing new to Monaco. The Ballets Russes, led by Serge Diaghilev in the early 1900s, drew thousands of patrons. The famous dancer Vaslav Nijinski was a regular performer in the early years of

Vaslav Nijinsky was a
featured dancer in many
of Monaco's ballets.

the company in Monaco. His name is attached to awards presented to the best entertainers at the Monaco Dance Forum, held every other December and featuring the world's most notable dance companies. Keeping in step with this fabulous heritage, Princess Caroline formed the New Ballet of Monte Carlo in 1985. Since then, audiences have been delighted by the dazzling performances of Serge Lifar, Alicia Alonso, and many other international stars.

Dancers perform modern dance at the New Ballet of Monte Carlo.

Princess Grace Foundation

In the United States, the Princess Grace Foundation–USA helps aspiring American artists and performers. It is based in New York City. Each year since 1984, the foundation has presented Princess Grace Awards for excellence in film, dance, and theater. In that time, more than $3 million has been given to 350 artists at more than 100 schools nationwide. In 2003, twenty emerging young artists received awards, including those who captured the highest award, the Princess Grace Statue.

Throughout the year, music-mad Monaco hosts numerous concerts, such as "Jazz on the Rock" in September. Since Monaco is such an exotic place to visit, the country also hosts myriad awards ceremonies. The annual World Music Awards attract the best-selling recording artists of the world, who gather for a star-filled program.

Singer Alicia Keys receives her award at the World Music Awards in Monaco.

Little Singers of Monaco

During the reign of Prince Antoine I in the early eighteenth century, a group of children were organized into a choir to sing liturgies in the Palatine Chapel. In 1973 another choir of boys (*Les Petits Chanteurs de Monaco*) was assembled to act as Monaco's child envoys. The group of twenty-six young performers now sings all over the world on concert tours twice a year. Prince Rainier III calls them "my little singing ambassadors." The group consists of boys from France, Italy, and Monaco. They have to pass rigorous exams to be admitted into the ensemble. This is a very prestigious ensemble and many hope to join its ranks.

Elephants and their trainers perform before large crowds at the International Circus Festival held in Monaco every January.

The Circus Takes Center Ring

More than 100 performers are invited to compete each January at Monaco's exciting International Circus Festival. The star-studded program is held under a huge canvas tent in the Fontvieille area, with seating around the center ring for more than 4,000 spectators. The event's Clown of Gold (*Clown d'Or*) award is considered the highest honor in the circus world. The Flying Pages, a troupe from Sarasota, Florida, won the festival's bronze award in 2002 for its skilled trapeze work. Circus-savvy twelve-year-old Anthony Page also captured a trophy as one of the top juvenile performers at the festival.

Monégasques' love affair with the circus extends to the arts. Circus Days (*Jours de Cirque*) was the hit of Monaco's 2002 gallery season. The show at the Grimaldi Forum was a collaboration between the principality and the National Museum of Popular Arts and Traditions in Paris. The exhibit showcased 250 displays, including a dozen circus trailers, parade floats, model circuses, posters, and related artifacts telling the circus story. Several antique wagons from the Circus World Museum in Baraboo, Wisconsin, were included in the show. In addition, European and American museums and private collectors contributed major works of art depicting the circus by such masters as Pablo Picasso, Henri de Toulouse-Lautrec, Fernand Léger, Georges Rouault, Marc Chagall, Albert Gleizes, and Henri Matisse. The show complemented the annual Monte Carlo Spring Arts Festival, bringing notable international artists from around the globe to showcase their paintings, music, theater, and dance.

Crafty Monégasques

Princess Grace appreciated the craftsmanship of her Monégasque subjects. The Princess Grace Foundation supports their work. Helped by these funds, painters, potters, and other specialists now have the time to develop their skills. They sell their jewelry, embroidery, and similar items in two shops in Monte Carlo, each called the *Boutique du Rocher*. Visitors love browsing amid the shelves and racks, admiring the displays before selecting a souvenir to take home. They make wonderful mememtoes of a trip to Monaco.

Racing at the Monaco Grand Prix

Alexandre Noghés, whose family were wealthy cigarette manufacturers, was a close friend of the Grimaldis. He became president of the local sports car and cycling club in 1909. He decided that a car rally was just what Monaco needed to attract even more of the rich and famous to Monte Carlo. The first race he organized, in 1909, included twenty-three cars

Start of the inaugural Monaco Grand Prix, 1929

and was won by Frenchman Henri Rougier driving a Turcat-Méry, doing an average of 6.2 miles per hour (10 km/hr). Competitors began the race in different places all around Europe and ended by converging in the streets of the city.

However, it was not until 1928 that Alexandre's son, Anthony, put forth the idea that the event should become a proper Grand Prix race. The idea subsequently received the enthusiastic support of Prince Louis II.

In 1929 the first Monaco Grand Prix was held. Today's race consists of seventy-

Drivers negotiate sharp
curves in Monaco's Formula
One Grand Prix, June 2003.

eight laps over a winding 2.1-mile (3.3-km) course past the casino, through a highway tunnel, and around the swimming pool by the port in La Condamine. Viewing stands are erected, including some built out in the harbor over the water. To protect their hearing, many bystanders wear earplugs.

Off to a Fast Start

"Grand Prix" is the term for a race that features Formula One race cars (below). These are technically intricate, high-powered Ferraris, Mercedes, Porsches, and other famous vehicles. All Grand Prix races are endorsed by the Federation Internationale de l'Automobile (FIA). Currently, more than fourteen countries around the world sponsor Grand Prix events, making them the most widely recognized auto races in the world.

In 1929 a reporter for the magazine *La Vie Automobile* observed the first Monaco Grand Prix and declared, "It goes without saying that the track is made up entirely of bends, steep uphill climbs, and fast downhill runs. Any respectable traffic system would have covered the track with 'Danger' signposts left, right, and center."

Since that first run in 1929, the fastest average speed at the Monaco race has advanced from its original record of about 50 miles per hour (80.5 km/hr) to about 88 miles per hour (141.6 km/hr). The cars speed so fast. They are almost a blur.

A prime spot to view this race is right at the start (*le Départ*) near one of the most dangerous bends on the course, called the Virage Sainte Dévote. Here, drivers often have accidents while they fight for a good position in the pack of cars as they zoom ahead.

Obviously, there is never a slow time in Monaco when it comes to athletics. Prince Rainier III has even said that "to be a good Monégasque, you must enjoy sport." The futuristic-looking Louis II Stadium in Fontvieille is home to the European Junior and French First Division football matches. Of course, in Monaco, "football" means soccer. The 20,000-seat stadium was dedicated in 1985 and is home to the Monégasque national team, proudly wearing their red-and-

Soccer matches are held in the 20,000-seat Louis II Stadium.

Tennis fans pack the Monte Carlo Country Club to watch the tennis open.

white uniforms. The facility also has basketball courts and Olympic-size swimming and diving pools.

Soccer is not the only sport played in Monaco. Major international golf tournaments such as the Monte Carlo Invitational Pro-Celebrity Golf Tournament are held on the rolling greens of the Monte Carlo Golf Club. The Monte Carlo Tennis Open takes place at the Monte Carlo Country Club.

Honoring the World's Athletes

Hollywood movie stars mingled with the sporting world's elite at the Laureus World Sports Awards in Monaco in May 2002. Considered to be the athletic world's equivalent to the movies' Oscars, the event attracted film stars Michael Douglas and Catherine Zeta-Jones, Sean Connery, and Morgan Freeman plus a bevy of supermodels. Prince Albert of Monaco hosted the event, where top honors went to auto racer Michael Schumacher and tennis star Jennifer Capriati. The two were named Sportsman and Sportswoman of the Year. The annual ceremony in Monaco was started in 2000 to celebrate global sporting excellence.

Monaco's Almost-National Sport

Boules, also known as *pétanque*, is often considered Monaco's national sport. The game, which is also played throughout southern France, is similar to British lawn bowling or Italian *boccie*. However, the Monégasque version is usually played with metal balls on a dirt surface beneath stately trees. When adults compete, they often sip from a glass of heady liquor called *pastis* to make a match a truly lively sport.

The balls weigh from 1 pound 7 ounces to 1 pound, 12 ounces (652 to 794 grams) and are from 2.78 to 3.15 inches (70.5 to 80 mm) in diameter. A player who specializes in pointing (or placing) uses a small, heavy boule. A shooter chooses a lighter boule. The object of the game is to toss the balls with a backspin so that they land closer to the small object ball (a *cochonnet*) than those of an opponent. Players also try to hit the object ball and knock it over to their balls and away from those of other players.

In 1958 Monaco was one of seven nations organizing an international federation of pétanque associations. Currently the organization has 600,000 licensed players in forty-six countries, including the United States and Canada. The 2001 world championship was held in Monaco. Monégasques play their *boules* at the Rainier III Boules Stadium in Fontvieille or at smaller courts scattered throughout Monte Carlo.

This tourney ranks as one of nine not-to-be-missed tennis tournaments in the world. There are also squash tourneys, cycle races, the International Rhythmic and Sports Gymnastics competitions, beach volleyball, water-polo matches, handball, regattas and other sailing races, and boxing matches. World swimming records have been set at the Rainier III Nautical Stadium near the port. Swimming greats such as French stars Alain Mosconi and Alex Jany have been among the competitors.

The Service of National Education, Youth and Sports, which is under the management of Monaco's Department of the Interior, oversees the twenty sports federations and fifty associations located in Monaco. Many receive government grants to help with their operations and belong to the Monaco Sports Association (ASM). These groups range from the Monaco Rifle Club to the Archery Company, the Cycling Union, and the Société Nautique de Monaco (for rowers).

The Monégasque Olympic Committee was formed in 1907 to oversee its member groups in shooting, basketball, cycling, fencing, gymnastics, judo, sailing, skiing, swimming, tennis, volleyball, and bobsledding. Several international sports groups are also headquartered in Monaco. They include the General Association of International Sports Federations (GAISF) and the International Association for Sport Without Violence, of which Prince Rainier III has been president. In 1994 the International Association of Athletics Federation (IAAF) moved its headquarters from London to Monaco.

A Lazy Summer Day

THIS IS GOING TO BE A GREAT DAY, THOUGHT ALFREDO Vergé as he opened one eye and looked out the window toward the Mediterranean Sea. The morning breeze brushed by the lace curtains made by his *grand-mére* (grandmother) Celestine when she was just a young girl. That was a long time before she married *grand-pére* (grandfather) Jacques, whose flaring mustache and stern look were captured in the photograph atop the piano in the living room. His mom's folks lived near the Exotic Garden, across Monte Carlo from Alfredo's home. Alfredo's other grandparents were already deceased. He missed them, especially around holiday time.

Alfredo heard the business report on the radio from the downstairs kitchen. Time for breakfast. His mother, Marie, would be setting out a basket of fresh croissants and *pain au chocolat*, buttery buns filled with a thin layer of delicious chocolate paste. She had been up early to go to the neighborhood bakery (*la boulangerie*) run by Pierre Girond. His tiny shop was the heart and soul of Alfredo's Monégasque neighborhood. Most of the locals visited Monsieur

Opposite: **Watching boats during Classic Week in Monaco**

Freshly baked bread and pastries help start the day in Monaco.

Girond's shop at least once a day. In the morning he did a brisk business in the breads and pastries that he had been working on since midnight.

A tall glass of freshly squeezed juice from oranges (*jus d' orange*) that Alfredo's mother purchased yesterday in the *marché*, the market, was waiting for him. A bowl of dark red cherries was on the counter. The oranges were from Spain, and the cherries came from neighboring France. Alfredo knew the cherries were there. The previous night, he had secretly swiped a few for a snack before going to bed.

Cherries from France are a favorite in Monaco.

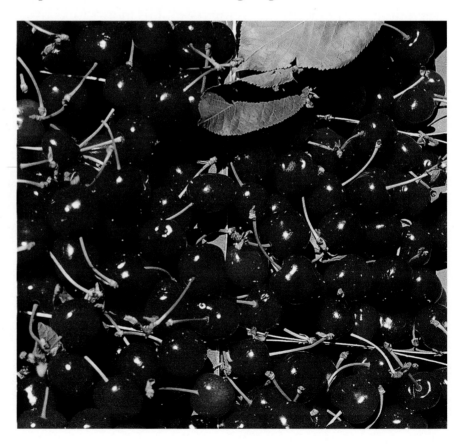

Monaco National Day

Monaco celebrates National Day (also known as *La Féte du Prince*) on November 19. Fireworks explode over the harbor the evening before, and a morning mass is celebrated in the cathedral. In addition, the festivities mark the prince's saint's day. Rainier is the thirtieth ruling prince of Monaco.

Taking His Time

Since it was summer and he was on holiday from his classes at Lycée Albert I, Alfredo could take his time rolling out from underneath the sheets. Alfredo did have one chore that day, however. He was going down to Monaco-Ville to help Madame Mouncoutie lay out some new items in her shop near the palace that sold Grand Prix souvenirs and Ferrari race car items. Madame and his mother were good friends from their university days in Paris.

After working, Alfredo planned on spending the afternoon with his friends. That evening the family was eager to watch some of the International Fireworks Festival, held in Monaco each July and August since 1966.

Alfredo was about to roll over one more time, ready to bury his head into the pillow. But his dog, Jacques, bounded into his room and jumped on the bed, immediately beginning to lick his left ear. His mother had sent the small bundle of fur and slurpy tongue to warn him that it was time really to get going for the day. Alfredo's father, Charles, had already left to catch the bus for work. He was the vice president in a bank that managed accounts from patrons around the world. Sometimes Charles Vergé needed to make business trips and was able to take his family with him. Alfredo had already been to London, Boston, Miami, and Quebec, as well as to South Africa and Finland. He loved traveling. Alfredo's older sister, Aimée, was not at home this summer. She was a management intern at a restaurant in Lyon, a city in France that was several hours north of Monte Carlo. Aimée hoped to open her own café someday and was studying hospitality management at the technical college in Monaco.

Jacques didn't give Alfredo much of a chance to think about vacations away from Monaco. The outside sunlight was already bouncing off his poster-covered walls. Alfredo had a spread of pictures depicting the French national soccer team that had participated in the World Cup championships in Korea and Japan. Like his pals, he was disappointed when the team lost out in the early rounds of play. He and his dad had

The French national soccer team poses for a group photo before the World Cup finals in 2002.

stayed up well into the early hours of the morning to watch the televised broadcasts from halfway around the world. But it was okay with him when the Brazilians finally won the championship. Football was football and always fun to watch. Alfredo hoped that maybe someday Monaco's team would qualify. He was too young to remember when the team was a semifinalist in the 1990 French football championships. Alfredo also spent a lot of time on his computer, checking soccer Web sites.

But today he would be late for his job at the shop if he didn't begin moving. Madame Mouncoutie didn't like him to be tardy. The store had to be open and ready for customers by midmorning. He brushed his teeth, put on clean blue shorts and a red-and-white-striped shirt, slipped into his sandals, and dashed downstairs with the dog in pursuit. "*Bonjour, Mama,*" he said between gulps of the delicious juice. She smiled back. With a table knife, he scooped a large helping of *miel* (honey) on his croissant. The sticky sweetness, with its touch of flowering lavender, was delicious.

After another quick toothbrushing, a face washing, and a scratch behind the ears for Jacques Alfredo was out the door and dashing down the steep hillside toward the bus stop. As he left, he yelled a Monégasque goodbye ("*a se revede!*") to his mom. He ran past Monsieur Girond's bakery and waved to Madame Robic, owner of the *tabac* next door, the newsstand overflowing with the bright covers of the French-language *La Gazette de Monaco*, *Monaco Actualités*, *Monaco Hebdo*, *Monaco Économie*, *Monaco Méditerranée Magazine*, and *Métropole*.

Copies of *The International Herald Tribune* were also displayed, along with a clutter of paperback novels, sports papers, maps, lotto (raffle) tickets, chewing gum, and cigarettes. His father and mother regularly read the English-language *Herald*

Bake Me Some Bread

Bread is always served with meals in Monaco, but not the large sandwich loaves that are typical of America and Canada. The Monégasques, like the French, prefer long, cylindrical breads with crisp crusts that resemble batons, known as *baguettes*. But there is a diversity of sizes and shapes from which to choose: the thin sticks known as *ficelles* (strings), the pointy-ended, chewy *bannettes*, and the extra-large baguettes known as the "restaurants."

Each has its devoted fans. But on one thing everyone agrees: Bread must be served fresh. Bread is never put in a bag but rather is given to the customer with a twist of paper around its middle for carrying. Nothing must ever compromise the fresh, oven-baked, chewy goodness. From the bakery directly to the table—that is the Monégasque tradition.

Tribune, as well as a regional French newspaper, *Nice-Matin*, which publishes a Monaco edition. As a financial expert, Monsieur Vergé had to keep up with political and economic events around the globe. He spoke fluent English, French, Italian, and Spanish, as well as some Arabic. Alfredo already could speak English well, in addition to his native French and Monégasque. He was also learning German in school.

Monaco Morning Comes Alive

Monaco comes to life as shops and cafés open for the day.

As Alfredo rode along toward Monaco-Ville, he watched the morning come alive. The Casino Square and adjacent streets

Moored yachts in Monaco's harbor bob at anchor.

were already bustling. He looked in the windows of such jewelers as Van Cleef and Arpels. He watched the shopkeepers at
Hermès, Céline, Saint Laurent, Rive Gauche, and Louis
Vuitton. Even the antiques dealers and interior decorators
were up and moving at Fersen and Adriano Ribolzi. Some
tourists were already walking around with their cameras. They
were happy finding a good place to park in one of Monaco's
cavernous underground garages.

Alfredo's bus rolled past the harbor and began its ascent
up the hill toward the palace. Deckhands in their white uniforms washed down the huge yachts bobbing in the harbor.

Going to School in Monaco

There are ten public schools in Monaco. Of these, seven are kindergarten and primary schools. There is one junior high school for pupils up to fifteen years old, one general and technical senior high school for pupils over fifteen, and one professional and hotel technical school. About 4,400 young people attend school each year. Three other schools are private, working under state contracts, serving around 1,500 students from kindergarten to senior high each year. The State Education Department employs 740 civil servants. Of these, 408 are teachers. The Catholic Church is responsible for several of the primary schools. For instance, Princess Stephanie attended a convent school called Les Dames de Saint Maur.

Children must attend school in Monaco from ages six to sixteen. Youngsters take the same classes as in France, but their history courses concentrate on Monaco. In their government classes young Monégasques learn about the heritage of the Grimaldi family dynasty.

Charles III College is more like a junior high school in the North American sense of the term. It prepares children to go on to higher studies. Secondary schooling is undertaken in the Lycée Albert I, where students receive diplomas in general education. They can also attend more classes at the lycée or at the Technical Lycée of Monte Carlo for instruction in hotel management, commerce, and specialized education. Other institutions include the Rainier III Academy of Music, the Princess Grace Academy of Classical Dance, the Municipal School of Plastic Arts, and a nursing school at the Princess Grace hospital.

To go on to higher education, pupils must pass a *baccalauréat* exam when they are sixteen years old. Only then can Monégasque youngsters attend French universities. Most graduates return to good-paying jobs in Monaco. Monégasques have one of the highest literacy rates in the world. Almost 100 percent can read and write.

A friend of Alfredo's dad, Monsieur Sastre, had a sailboat moored there and sometimes gave the Vergés a ride out on the Mediterranean.

A few weeks earlier they had sailed to Saint-Tropez along the French Riviera and had lunch in an outdoor restaurant in the sprawling port city. Even Jacques came on the daylong cruise, enjoying the sea wind spraying his whiskers. Alfredo ate a full platter of a pesto gnocchi, a chunky oval-shaped pasta made from potatoes flavored with basil. He topped off the meal with a sweet fruit tart (*les tartlettes aux fruits du temps*) made from fresh raspberries, bananas, and strawberries. Mmmm, good.

By the end of that meal Alfredo was full. His mom and dad, the Sastres, and several of their friends who had sailed with them wanted to watch the boules games in the plaza fronting their table. That was okay with Alfredo. It was hilarious to observe the loud debating and waving of arms. Players carefully used tape measures to settle arguments as to which of two boules was closer to the cochonnet, the target ball.

Alfredo also appreciated that there were plenty of pretty girls strolling past his vantage point. Many were shopping at the fancy clothing stores near the restaurant. He thought some looked like recording stars, but he wasn't sure.

Then it was time to return home. As the sun dipped into the western Mediterranean, the sailboat arrived back at Monaco. Alfredo helped ready the vessel for docking. That night he barely made it to his bed before falling asleep.

Shop Displays

At his bus stop, Alfredo hopped off and ran down the narrow street to the souvenir shop. *"Bonjour, Madame! Comment allez-vous?"* ("Hello, Madame! How are you?"), he said politely in French. *"Bien, bien,"* ("Well, well") she replied with a wide smile. Alfredo spent the rest of the morning unpacking and laying out red shirts adorned with the Ferrari racing-car logo. Madame showed him how to arrange the displays so that they would catch the visitors' eyes. Alfredo loved watching the

A shop displays racing items for fans to purchase.

Grand Prix auto race, especially when the high-powered cars squealed around the tight La Racasse hairpin bend. Monsieur Vergé always had tickets to the event because of his position at the bank. Looking over the stock of clothing in the shop, Alfredo wondered how he might look in a race driver's uniform.

Once his job was done for the day and he was dismissed by Madame, Alfredo zipped into a nearby restaurant for a quick lunch of freshly caught mussels and crispy French fries (*pomme frites*). He then galloped off to catch another bus and meet his school buddies Karl, Gino, and Eddie outside the Louis II Stadium. They hoped to catch a glimpse of AS Monaco, the national football (soccer) team, heading to practice. He and his pals played for their school team and attended almost every home match in the stadium, cheering for the "Barbagiuans." (The nickname refers to a popular

Monégasque dish of ravioli stuffed with orange squash.) On days like this, when there were a lot of things to do, Alfredo was glad that Monaco was compact and easy to navigate.

The boys watched the players enter the stadium and waved to their heroes. They then wandered down to the Quai Jean-Charles Rey, a street near the harbor, to see if any fancy new yachts had entered the Port of Fontvieille. They sat on a bench under the shade of a palm tree near the water and argued about the struggling Monaco team and who might make a good team manager. They were all disappointed in Didier Deschamps, who had coached the Monégasques for

Reviving Traditions

The National Committee of Monégasque Traditions, established in 1924, is attempting to resurrect many old ceremonies. On most days Monégasques dress in regular modern clothes. But on holidays many of the women choose to wear peasant costumes similar to those worn in southern France. Lace veils are often accented with a rose or another flower. A full skirt with a dark apron and a white blouse completes the outfit. Men favor knee pants, with colorful sashes wrapped around their waists and string ties around their neck.

several seasons. Deschamps, the former captain of the French team that captured the World Cup in 1998, always seemed to be arguing with his players and the club officials.

The conversation rolled around to the Tour de France, a world-famous bike race. The event looped more than 2,000 miles (3,219 km) through Luxembourg and Germany, as well as in France. Alfredo recently had invited his friends to his house to watch the conclusion of the 100-year-old sporting event. The race was regularly televised in Monaco, and the boys wanted to see the final minutes as American Lance Armstrong won his fifth title. The kids cheered and toasted the victory with their sodas. When he jumped up, Eddie spilled a bowl of potato chips, much to Jacque's delight.

Now, as they half-dozed by the harbor, the boys discussed Armstrong's latest win, tying the record of five victories. Among the previous victors was Jacques Anquetil of France, who captured titles in 1957 and from 1961 to 1964. Karl and Eddie figured Armstrong eventually could take an unheard-of six wins. Gino and Alfredo had their doubts.

On the way back up the harbor to the bus for the ride home, they stopped at a concession stand for a *glâce*, a heavy ice cream. Alfredo liked his cool snack since it included fresh fruit. When he returned to his house, it was almost time for supper. His mom was talking on the phone with Aimée, who was excited that several American film stars had stopped for lunch at the restaurant in Lyon where she was working.

Soon his father would be home and the family could sit down on their patio overlooking the city, have a light supper,

and then watch the International Fireworks Festival. Madame Vergé prepared fresh salmon, creamy macaroni, and a large salad of greens and tomatoes, one of Alfredo's favorite meals. Jacques gnawed on a new bone secured that day from the butcher at the foot of the hill.

As night descended on the city, thousands of lights twinkled across the horizon. Even the trees on the esplanade far below the Vergés' house were draped with bright fairyland necklaces. Monaco was aglow. As the fireworks roared skyward from the vicinity of the breakwater separating the harbor from the sea, Jacque's ears perked up. But the small dog didn't pause in his bone chewing.

Alfredo yawned. It was time to call it a day.

Fireworks light up the Monaco sky.

Timeline

Monaco's History		World History	
		2500 B.C.	Egyptians build the Pyramids and the Sphinx in Giza.
		563 B.C.	The Buddha is born in India.
Emperor Diocletian persecutes Christians. Saint Dévote is martyred.	A.D. 303–304	A.D. 313	The Roman emperor Constantine recognizes Christianity.
Saracens from North Africa control Monaco coast.	6th–10th century	610	The Prophet Muhammad begins preaching a new religion called Islam.
		1054	The Eastern (Orthodox) and Western (Roman) Churches break apart.
		1066	William the Conqueror defeats the English in the Battle of Hastings.
		1095	Pope Urban II proclaims the First Crusade.
Emperor Henry VI grants authority over Monaco to the Genovese.	1191		
Genovese settle on The Rock and build a fort.	1215	1215	King John seals the Magna Carta.
Disguised as a monk, François Grimaldi captures fortress of Monaco.	1297		
		1300s	The Renaissance begins in Italy.
		1347	The Black Death sweeps through Europe.
		1453	Ottoman Turks capture Constantinople, conquering the Byzantine Empire.
Charles VIII of France recognizes independence of Monaco.	1489	1492	Columbus arrives in North America.
Monaco placed under protection of Spain.	1524	1500s	The Reformation leads to the birth of Protestantism.
Honoré II takes the title of prince of Monaco.	1614		
		1776	The Declaration of Independence is signed.
Monaco attached to the French Republic under the name of Fort Hercules.	1793	1789	The French Revolution begins.
Treaty of Paris gives Sardinia sovereignty over Monaco.	1815		
Charles III gives to France his rights over Menton and Roquebrune in order to guarantee independence of Monaco.	1861		

Monaco's History

Casino gambling starts in Monaco.	1863
Spelugues district becomes Monte Carlo.	1866
Monaco issues its first postage stamp.	1885
Albert I founds Anthropological Museum.	1902
First Monaco Grand Prix held.	1929
Exotic Garden opens.	1933
Radio Monte Carlo launched.	1942
Prince Rainier III ascends to throne.	1949
Zoological Garden founded.	1954
Rainier marries American Grace Kelly.	1956
Princess Caroline born; explorer Jacques-Yves Cousteau becomes director of Oceanographic Museum.	1957
Prince Albert born.	1958
Princess Grace Foundation established.	1964
Princess Stephanie born.	1965
International Circus Festival founded.	1974
Princess Grace dies after an auto crash.	1982
Monaco joins the United Nations.	1993
Appeals court upholds Monaco's first conviction of money laundering.	1998
Monaco begins using the euro as the base unit of currency; major circus exhibit opens at the Grimaldi Forum Monaco.	2002

World History

1865	The American Civil War ends.
1914	World War I breaks out.
1917	The Bolshevik Revolution brings communism to Russia.
1929	Worldwide economic depression begins.
1939	World War II begins, following the German invasion of Poland.
1945	World War II ends.
1957	The Vietnam War starts.
1969	Humans land on the moon.
1975	The Vietnam War ends.
1979	Soviet Union invades Afghanistan.
1983	Drought and famine in Africa.
1989	The Berlin Wall is torn down as communism crumbles in Eastern Europe.
1991	Soviet Union breaks into separate states.
1992	Bill Clinton is elected U.S. president.
2000	George W. Bush is elected U.S. president.
2001	Terrorists attack World Trade Towers, New York, and the Pentagon, Washington, D.C.

Fast Facts

Official name: Principality of Monaco (*Principauté Monaco*)

Capital: Monaco-Ville

Monte Carlo

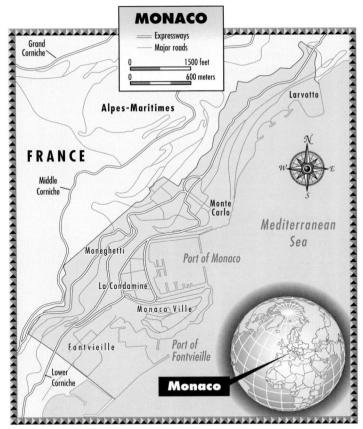

Monaco's flag

Port of Monaco

Official language:	French, though English, Italian, and Monégasque (a mixture of French and Italian) are widely spoken.
Official religion:	Roman Catholic
Government:	Constitutional monarchy
Head of state:	Prince Rainier III
Heir apparent:	Prince Albert Alexandre Louis Pierre, son of Prince Rainier III
Area:	0.76 square miles (1.97 sq km)
Length of border with France:	2.73 miles (4.4 km)
Length of coastline:	2.55 miles (4.1 km)
Lowest elevation:	Mediterranean coast: sea level
Highest elevation:	Mont Agel: 459 feet (140 m)
Climate:	Mild year-round; temperatures hover around 50°F (10°C) in January and 80°F (27°C) in July
Name of citizens:	Monégasques
National population (2001 est.):	32,020, 5,123 of whom are Monégasques
Ethnic population:	French 47%
	Italian 16%
	Monégasque 16%
	other 21%

Princess Grace Rose Garden

Famous landmarks: ▶ *The Grimaldi Palace*, Monaco-Ville

▶ *Oceanographic Museum*, Monaco-Ville

▶ *The Grand Casino*, Monte Carlo

▶ *Louis II Stadium*, Fontvieille

▶ *Exotic Garden*, Moneghetti

▶ *Monte Carlo Sporting Club*, Larvotto

Industry: Since it has no natural resources, Monaco must import its food and all raw products. It depends on tourism, construction, banking, chemicals, textiles, plastics, and printing for its revenue. Monaco attracts visitors to its gambling casinos, harbor, and historical sites, as well as to conventions, festivals, and major sporting events such as the Grand Prix auto race. Monaco is a world financial center, with numerous banks catering to accounts from around the globe.

Currency: The euro

Weights and measures: Metric system

Literacy: 99%

Currency

Traditional dress

Prince Rainier III

Common words and phrases:	Monégasque	English
	Salve	Hello
	A se revede	Goodbye
	Sciá or *Madama*	Madam
	Sciu or *Monsue*	Sir
	Me ciamu	My name is
	Sci	Yes
	Mercí	Thank you
	Pe pieijé	Please

Famous Monégasques:		
	Antoine I *Soldier*	(1661–1731)
	Léo Albert C.A. Ferré *Poet, composer, singer*	(1916–1993)
	Louis I *Diplomat*	(1642–1701)
	Louis Notari *Writer*	(1879–1961)
	Prince Albert I *Explorer, scientist, ruler of Monaco*	(1848–1922)
	Prince Albert *Son of Prince Rainier III, heir to the throne*	(1958–)
	Princess Grace *Former movie star, wife of Rainier III*	(1929–1982)
	Prince Rainier III *Ruler of Monaco*	(1923–)

To Find Out More

Nonfiction

▶ Black, Loraine. *Let's Visit Monaco*. London: Burke, 1984.

▶ Campbell, Siri. *Inside Monaco*. Glen Ellyn, Ill.: MCI Publishing, 1996.

▶ *All the Principality of Monaco*. Barcelona: Editions Molipor, Editorial Escudo De Oro, SA.

▶ St. John, Jetty. *Monaco Grand Prix*. Minneapolis: Lerner Publications Co., 1989.

Web Sites

▶ **Monaco Government Tourist Office**
http:/www.visitmonaco.com
Contains information about Monaco, including travel and economic details, and links to other sites about the country.

▶ **CIA World Fact Book**
http://www.odci.gov/
Search for Monaco from the home page. Provides up-to-date geographic, financial, government, and social information about Monaco.

Organizations

▶ **Monaco Government Tourist Office**
565 Fifth Avenue
New York, NY 10017
(800) 753-9696 or
mgto@monaco1.org
www.visitmonaco.com

▶ **Consulate General of Monaco**
565 Fifth Avenue
New York, NY 10017
212-286-0500
info@monaco-consulate.com
www.monaco-consulate.com

Index

Page numbers in *italics* indicate illustrations.

police, 56, *56*
pollution, 21
population, 77
postage stamps, 69, *69*
Princely Palace, *10*, 17, *44*, 50, *50*
Prince Pierre Foundation, 93
Princess Grace
 Dance Academy, 93
 Foundation, 93, 100
 Hospital, 50, *79*
 Rose Garden, *26*
promogeniture, 45, 47

R
Radio Monte Carlo (RMC), 73
railroads, 65
railways, 61
Rainier III. *See* Grimaldi, Rainier III
religion
 Christian persecution, 81
 freedom of worship, 87–88
 Jewish, 85

Protestant, 85
Roman Catholic, 84
Saint Dévote, 81–84, *82*
traditions and holidays, 83, 88–91
Republic of Genoa, 35
restaurants, 66, *73*
revolts/uprisings
 Menton and Roquebrune in 1848, 39
 threat in 1800s, 60–61
roadways, 19, *19*, 61
Rock, The, 17
Rougier, Henri, 104

S
sailors, 9
Saint Dévote, 81–84, *82*
Saint Dévote Chapel, *84*
Saint John's Day, 89–91
Saint Nicholas, 85
Saint Roman, 89, *89*
Saracen on horseback (fresco), *34*
Sardinia, 38–39

Meet the Author

MARTIN HINTZ has written several dozen titles for the Enchantment of the World series. To research for Monaco, he used the Internet, libraries, magazine articles and newspapers, interviewed Monégasques, and, of course, toured their wonderful country.

In addition to writing for Children's Press, Hintz is a well-known travel writer in other venues. He has produced hundreds of magazine and newspaper articles on international and stateside destinations, as well as stories on the tourism business, security, and other issues related to travel.

Hintz has almost 100 books to his credit for a wide range of publishers. Among them is a book on Prohibition, two on the circus, and four on drag racing. He also puts out *The Irish American Post*, a news magazine that went totally online in 2001 after ten years as a print publication. In addition, he directs the Mountjoy Writers Group, an international news syndicate. In this capacity he works with journalists in Japan, India, Canada, Britain, Ireland, the United States, and Mexico.

He is active in numerous journalism associations, including serving as chairman of the board and immediate past president of the Society of American Travel Writers. He is a member of the international committee of the Society of Professional Journalists and belongs to the Committee to Protect Journalists, a watchdog association that keeps track of journalists in trouble with their governments. Hintz is also a member of his local library board.

He and his wife, Pam, travel extensively and have often visited France and Italy, which are Monaco's neighbors. While in Monaco, they peeked into the casino, watched the changing of the palace guard, gawked at the fish in the Oceanographic Institute, wandered the streets of the city, and admired the yachts docked in the Monte Carlo harbor.

Living on a small farm north of Milwaukee, Wisconsin, the couple raises chickens, including a French breed. They once had a very large pig named Porcine (the French word for "pig"), which often sat on their front porch. Porcine also loved racing alongside the lawn mower when Hintz did his yard chores.

Photo Credits